Queen Amang
the Heather

Queen Amang the Heather

The Life of Belle Stewart

Sheila Stewart, MBE

BIRLINN

First published in Great Britain in 2006 by
Birlinn Limited
West Newington House
10 Newington Road
Edinburgh
EH9 1QS

www.birlinn.co.uk

Reprinted 2007, 2008, 2011

ISBN: 978 1 84158 528 4

British Library Cataloguing-in-Publication Data
A catalogue record for this book is available from the
British Library

Typeset by Textype, Cambridge
Music typeset by John Hearne
Printed and bound by Cox & Wyman Ltd, Reading

Contents

Preface

When Sheila asked me to write this preface to her mother the first thing that sprang instantly to mind was how can I describe the voice of a song thrush singing a call of love to his mate? It can't be done without hearing for oneself the depth, the clarity and hauntingly beautiful notes of Mother Nature's small, insignificant feathered creature.

She was born on a midsummer day in a bowed tent, beside a farm. Her newborn cries joined those of plovers, oystercatchers and lapwing chicks. Claypotts was the name of the farm on the outskirts of the peaceful village of Caputh; a favoured spot for Perthshire's travelling tinkers.

Onto the road on her mother's back in a coarse woollen shawl snuggled the tiny baby. Nature's tuneful birds and the rhythmic tramping of her parents' feet on the old track roads instilled in bonnie Belle threads of music that soon were woven into a beautiful quilt of traditional ballads. As she grew into a strong-legged youngster and joined the walkers alongside the cartwheels and clipping hooves of the ponies that pulled them, she found and nurtured her own rhythms.

Belle gave her songs atmosphere; you listened and were transported into a gloaming where setting sun threw silhouettes of treetops to join and sway with an orange horizon. Her quirky tunes lifted your toes to tap them on whatever was handy; fingers danced to phantom acoustics where invisible piano keys jumped into life before your eyes.

Belle lived her emotions through song; she reared her children into those threads; brought her husband Alex along an ever-roaming road of music. To her, if it had substance it was a living tune. But what mattered most were the feelings. Her words were never minced: 'Dinna mak a fool o the sangs. Love them as if you yerself was living through them, and if ye love singing them, for God's sake dae it wi aa yer hert,' was her parting tip to budding singers anxious for important critique from the famous Belle.

If meeting Belle for the first time, her friendliness and warmth encircled you. No matter how full her house was with family, friends and folklorists, she gave you at that initial meeting her undivided attention. Next visit she would say a brief hello followed by, 'Ye ken whaur the kettle is fill a cup fir me tae.'

She knew you, so she trusted you: simple as that, another part of her constant string of guests tramping through the Stewarts o Blair's front room leaving with dreams of being a great folk singer or a balladeer like Belle. And that was what she did: instilled in individuals a sense of reaching to aspiring levels. However, and I can say this with the backing of dozens of successful singers, only one person has ever sat upon that elusive seat and this is Sheila, her prodigy.

One might think it an honour to be born with such tremendous qualities, but for a while during Sheila's early days, being the daughter of the 'Queen Amang the Heather' was to prove a curse.

Belle gave her best, nothing else was accepted; if she gave it, then so too must her daughter. Days and nights were a constant 'Don't sing like that. Why do you join words that must stay apart? Who told you to put that note in there? Keep the auld lilt, ye're a ballad singer and no a stiffent airn tree.' Little grasping her mother's determination for perfection and seeing her instead as a kind of 'dictator', Sheila would call Belle, under her breath, 'Mussolini' or, worse, 'Hitler'.

So, like many strictly schooled teenagers, there was a form of rebellion. But Belle's strong nature and adoration of her craft found the wayward daughter picking up her reins and falling back into line, with an in-depth knowledge that her road, like her mother's, had already been paved by ancestors. Blooming from a thorny bud into a beautiful rose, she went on to surpass and break her mother's mould.

As Scottish travellers, the entire family, and when Belle was in her prime there were four generations, was proud of their heritage. Belle and Alex had seven children (two died in infancy). They'd settled in Blairgowrie into a hostile environment, but that was nothing new to them. As wandering tinsmiths, their forebears were hounded and racially abused for hundreds of years. But as a unit, survival was foremost. They continued living in the small Perthshire town, opting to speak Cant rather than English, and apart from keeping on friendly terms with immediate neighbours, kept entirely to themselves.

Belle was eternally grateful to Hamish Henderson at the School of Scottish Studies, Ewan MacColl, Peggy Seeger and Peter Shepherd, to name a few, for opening a window to the world. An entire audience of folklorists, storytellers and balladeers owe much to hearing the Stewarts o Blair on radio, in concert and on television. Her dreams had come true to share her precious songs with everyone.

Alex, son of the legendary piper John Stewart, had inherited his own musical skills and, according to Hamish Henderson, could play hauntingly. Sheila, Cathie and several family members were recorded and also given a voice quite an achievement because, in Belle's own words: 'Settled folk are aye wanting tae git rid o' trevellers and tinkers, nae tae listen tae them singing and piping.'

But what she found out was instead of people perceiving the travellers as degenerates, they were held as the carrying stream of Scottish music, the kind that inspired Robbie Burns to put pen to paper hearing beggars and tinkers singing their old songs around the fire of the famous public house of Poosie Nancy. Soon every singer worth his salt was singing into microphones, recording Belle's tunes.

I will end this preface of the great Belle Stewart with a few poignant words from Hamish Henderson after attending Belle's funeral. He was talking old times with Sheila, and I quote: 'There are many musical branches to a tree but the travelling people are the roots.'

Jess Smith

Glossary

This is a selective glossary, which gives definitions of Scots and Cant words as they are used in the book.

airn tree: alder tree
barra: wheelbarrow
bing avree: go away
bing: heap, pile
birl: whirl around, dance
blaw: oatmeal
bobambie: uneducated person
cacavie: kettle
cantarach: form of mouth music
clip cloots wi: quarrel with; *tongue that wad clip cloots:* sharp tongue
clogger: dancer
cloot: piece of cloth, rag
clootie dumpling: dumpling wrapped in cloth and boiled
congnach: connected, spiritual sensation a musician feels and conveys to an audience when playing or singing from the heart and not from the head
cotter hoose: small cottage
coull: man
country hantle: non-traveller
crouse: cosy, comfortable
cull: stupid
cutty: pipe
dae a slide: run away
divots: mud and grass sods
drookerin: telling fortunes/reading palms

e'en: eyes
fankle: tangle
feart: afraid
fegs: goodness!
flattrin: fish
guddle: catch fish with one's hands
habben: food
intae our gowles: on our laps
jurival: genitals
kea laddie: jackdaw
lippin: depend, trust
lour: money
mallin promise: type of raspberry bush
moich: daft
mort: woman
moud: die
mouded: dead
naken: a traveller
owre: over
oxter: armpit, under part of the upper arm
plug: piece of tobacco
pockle: bagful, large number
puckle: small amount of something
quad: prison; *quadded*: sent or condemned to jail
reek: smoke
rickle: loose heap, rickety structure
roan: gutter
scull: wire mesh basket used for carrying potatoes, turnips etc.
shielin: small hut
Sheltie pony: Shetland pony
shew: sew
sib a freen: closely related
skean dhu: dirk or dagger, usually carried in the stocking
slab (Aberdeenshire): tea
sloosh: pee
slorach: mixed stew
smit: infect

stead: house
steading: farm buildings
stottin bits: loose bacon
trachle: struggle
wand: reed
wastins: tumble-down building
wean: child
weed (Perthshire): tea
whinny knowes: hills covered with gorse
whitterick: weasel
wime: tummy
yin: one

Queen Amang the Heather

Free rhythm ♩ = c.82

Noo, as I roved out one summer's day. A-mang lofty hills and moorland and moun-tain. It was there I spied the love-ly maid whilst I wi oth-ers was out a-hunt-ing.

Noo, as I roved out one summer's day,
Amang lofty hills and moorland and mountain
It was there I spied the lovely maid
Whilst I wi others was out a-hunting.

No shoes nor stockings did she wear
Neither had she a hat nor had she favour
But her golden locks aye and her ringlets rare
On the gentle breeze played aroun her shoulders.

'Oh,' I says, 'braw lassie why roam yir lane,
Why roam yir lane amang the heather?'
'Why,' she says, 'my faither's awa frae hame
And I'm herding aa his yowes thegither.'

Noo I says, 'Braw lassie if you'll be mine
And careless ye lie on a bed of feather,
In silks and satins you will shine
And you'll be my queen amang the heather.'

Noo she says, 'Kind sir, your offer is good
But I'm afraid it was meant for laughter
For I know you are some rich squire's son
And I'm a poor lame shepherd's dochter.

'Oh, but had ye been a shepherd loon
A-herding the yowes in yonder valley
Or had ye been a plooman's son
Wi all my hairt I would hae loo'ed ye.'

Noo, I hae been to balls and I hae been to halls
I've been in London and Balquhidder
But the bonniest lass that ever I did see
She was herding yowes amang the heather.

As we baith sat doon upon the plain
We sat a while and we talked thegither
And I left my yowes for to stray their lane
Til I wooed my queen amang the heather.

1906–1934

Some people are fortunate and are born with a silver spoon in their mouth, and reach the height of their ambition. On the other end of the scale of fortune, a child was born who rose to the highest level, and against all odds gave to the world the precious gift of her oral tradition, leaving behind a legacy belonging to travellers of a bygone age. Her great achievements were honoured by the award of a BEM from Her Majesty the Queen. This woman was my mother, Belle Stewart, née MacGregor, and this is her biography.

Belle was born in a bow tent on the banks of the River Tay on 18 July 1906 in a village called Caputh. The morning she was born, her father Donald MacGregor, known by all the travellers as Dan, was down at the river pearl-fishing. This is how the travellers made their money in the summertime, collecting pearls from freshwater mussels. Well, he fished all morning and at twelve noon he decided to come out of the water and open his shells. There was nothing in the first few dozen, but then from his bag he pulled out a large crook, a twisted shell, and inside it he found a beautiful pearl, about twenty grains, perfect and round.

After he found the pearl, he decided to fish a wee bit longer. Just then, the estate gilly came past in a rowing boat and approached the bank near to where he was fishing. 'Well,' said the gilly, 'any luck today, Dan?'

'Yes,' said my grandfather, 'I got a beauty this morning,' and he took the pearl out and showed it to him. There were two other people in the boat, an American couple, and they were introduced to my grandfather. At that moment, his son Donald came running up, very, very, excited.

'Daddy, Daddy! My mither has just had a wee girl!'

My grandfather already had two sons, so he was over the moon with his wee girl. 'Well,' he said to the gilly, 'that's two pearls I got today.' The American couple asked if they could buy the pearl from him. 'Yes,' he said, 'but not my wee lassie!'

They gave him five pounds for the pearl, which was a lot of money in 1906. He was the happiest and the proudest man that day. Little did he know he wouldn't live to enjoy his wee lassie for long.

Next day, the family packed up and headed for Braemar. Traveller women in those days never rested for long after they had their babies. They had no car, nor even a horse and cart then, so they put their belongings and the baby in a pram, tied tent sticks to the side of it and headed over the hill.

When they arrived in Braemar, my granny went to the hotel to see if she could beg some food, and the girl who came to the door knew her and was excited about the baby. She took it in to let the rest of the staff see it and was away for about twenty minutes.

When she came back, she had a big handful of sixpences. My granny was so pleased and thanked the maid for the staff's kindness.

Now, my mother's father was a wonderful singer, and travellers would travel for miles to camp beside him just to listen to him. They said he could sing the birds off the trees. When they left Braemar, the family headed for Blairgowrie and camped that night near the Devil's Elbow. There were two or three camps there of Whytes and Stewarts. They had been drinking all day and my grandfather knew they would torment him to sing to them, but the family were tired, so they put up their tent and stayed. A man, Duncan Stewart was his name, came over with a few other men and asked my grandfather to give them a song. 'I will,' he said, 'but I will have my tea first.'

'Tae hell wi the tea,' said Duncan. 'A song first.'

Dan knew he wasn't going to get out of this, so he started singing, but when they had heard one they wanted more. 'No,' he said, 'I am havin my tea.'

So they set about him and knocked him unconscious. He was out for about twenty minutes. When he came round and sat up, they were all gone, cleared out. Only my granny was still there, with the boys, her brother Jimmy Jack who lived with them and the baby – my mother. The men had wrecked everything belonging to the family and had torn up their tent and robbed them of all their money. They had nothing left.

So they put their bundles on their back, and my grandfather said, 'Come on Martha, we're headin to Blair.' They slept in hedges and among the heather for two days until they reached Blairgowrie.

When they arrived there, my granny went to see her cousin Agnes and told them all that had happened to them. Agnes said, 'I can give you a bite to eat, but you cannae stay wi me.' She gave them an old cover to make a tent and they pitched it down the Wellton Road about quarter of a mile out of town. She also gave them half a crown to buy food until they could get back on their feet – it was a godsend. They bought groceries with some of the money that day, but the next day my grandfather walked up to Blair. Now, he liked a wee dram, and he met some travellers and went to the pub with them. He went on a drinking spree for a few days, and my granny was left with the bairns and no food. She did the best she could.

Eventually he came home to the tent with one shilling in his pocket, and that fed them that night. Next morning, my granny asked him where he had been for two days. 'Oh,' he said, 'I was drinkin with the boys.' She later found out they were the same boys that had robbed them up in the glen.

You can imagine the row he got from her. He stayed off the drink for a few weeks after that to keep the peace. The next day he said, 'Martha, I think we will head to Alyth. It has always been good for us there.' So the following day they moved to Alyth, where he got work on the farms.

*

My mother was only nine months old when tragedy struck. By this time the family had managed to save up and they had a horse and cart, which made things a lot easier.

They had been up Glen Isla working on a farm, where my grandfather worked every year. The day he finished, the farmer had a wee party for the workers, and my grandfather got very drunk, and crawled his way home.

The next day they were moving down to Blairgowrie. They all got up and packed their things for the journey. My grandfather was leading the horse down the road when he shouted to my granny's brother, who was fifteen at the time, 'Jimmy, you will have to lead the horse, because I feel so ill after the drink last night. I am in the doldrums wi drink.' He climbed into the back of the cart to rest and have a wee sleep. Then they carried on down the road.

When they were nearing Alyth, Jimmy went to the back of the cart to rouse my grandfather, but he couldn't wake him. He had choked on his own vomit.

Jimmy ran to the shop where my granny was. She came running out with the shopkeeper and looked in the cart. 'Oh my God, Martha,' said the shopkeeper, 'Dan doesn't look well. You will have to take him to the doctor down the street.'

But when my granny went to the surgery, the doctor wouldn't let her in. He stretched my grandfather out in the coach shed and then went back into his office. It was a long time before he came back to look at him. After he had examined my grandfather, he turned to my granny and said, 'There is nothing I can do for this man. He is dead.' My granny stood there crying with my mother, a baby, in her arms.

It got back to my granny later that day that the doctor had said to Mr Edwards in the shop, 'Oh well, why worry? He was only a tinker.'

And so my mother never knew her father. He died at thirty-two. They took him to the police mortuary and he was buried from there in a pauper's grave.

Now my granny was left with three bairns to bring up on her own, so she headed to Blairgowrie to try and get money from the parish. They gave her a note for two shillings and sixpence to take to the grocer's shop because they never gave out money in those days. She bought her groceries and there was some money left over. My granny, like most travelling woman, enjoyed her pipe, so she said to the grocer, 'Can I please have tobacco for the rest of the money?'

Well, the man went mad at her! 'Don't you know', he said, 'tobacco is a luxury and is forbidden by the parish?' He made her take a pot of jam instead.

She had just lost her man and this is the way she was treated. Travelling people were not respected in those days; they were treated as if they were animals with no feelings. Mind you, the travellers themselves could be cruel too. When she got to Blairgowrie, my grandmother went to a traveller to try and sell her horse and cart. 'What?' said the traveller. 'Me buy that horse and cart? No way, not after a man died in it.' Eventually, a man in Blair called Mr Dall bought the horse and cart for three pounds. My grandfather had also been an excellent tinsmith, and Mr Dall bought all his tools for making tin.

Now my granny was left with an awful worry, because if a traveller woman was seen travelling with no husband, the authorities would take her children away from her and put them in a home. So she decided her wandering days were over.

She went to plant trees for a man named Lumpy McFarlane – the travellers called him that because he had a lump on his neck. He was the greediest man on earth. He worked the travellers to death, and paid them very little. Jimmy Jack and my mother's brother Donald got one shilling a day for tree-planting work, but my mother's brother Andy was too young to work. So he went hawking the houses round Glen Isla with my granny and my mother, who was then still just a babe in arms.

This went on till the berry time in Blair, when my granny went to see a solicitor there named Toby Dewar. He was a very decent man – if he had an empty house he would give it to a traveller. There was no class distinction with him and he treated all men as equal. So my granny got a house from him in Croft Lane, Blairgowrie at sixpence a week. My mother was a one-year-old when she moved into her first house, and from then on Blairgowrie was her home.

★

My mother grew up to be a bonnie girl. She had very curly hair with masses of ringlets and she was very slim. She was adored by her uncle Jimmy and her two brothers.

'Mammy,' she said one day, 'what happened to my daddy?' Her mother told her everything that she thought she could handle at that age, but her father's death remained a terrible void in her life. Her mother also told her all about her granny and grandfather. Her granny was called Wee Betty MacPhee. A story about her stuck in my mother's mind all her life, and she told it to me.

The incident happened at Glenisla Games above Kirriemuir, which were very popular at the time. In those days, the games were called a friendly society and this was kept up by all the gentry.

My mother's granny Wee Betty always liked a wee dram. At the Glenisla Games one day, she got talking to two farmers who had heard she could dance but had never seen her do so.

'Yes, I can dance,' she said, so they challenged her to dance on the stage in public and they bet her a bottle of whisky and five shillings. So she consented and said she would do the sword dance, but that she wouldn't use swords. Instead, she would do it with twenty-four glasses of water. They sent for the tumblers and made a cross, like swords, and filled the glasses up with water. Now, the sword dance then was an art and you weren't allowed to look at your feet while dancing. Wee Betty danced the sword dance over the glasses, and never spilled a drop of water. The spectators who watched her thought she was great – they had never seen this done before. The person who was most amazed by her dancing was the piper who played for her. 'I have never seen the likes of that before,' he said, 'and perhaps I never will again. It was a bet well earned.' So she got her bottle of whisky and her five shillings.

Not long afterwards, she met an awful death. She had been drinking in an inn in New Alyth and staggered out and collapsed in the inn's forecourt. Now, a farmer was coming home from the cattle market in Blairgowrie with his horse and cart, and he pulled into the inn for a drink on his way home. He didn't see her and ran right over her shoulders and chest with the big iron wheels of the cart. The farmer went into the inn and said, 'I think I have just run over somebody.'

They ran out of the inn and found her lying there. 'Oh my dear God,' someone said, 'it's Betty MacPhee – she left here only a wee while ago.'

The man who had run her over said, 'Och, these damn tinkers are everywhere. She got what she deserved – they are never off the road.'

There were two missionary women who lived at that time in New Alyth, and they took Betty in to nurse her, but she died during the night. She had her wee clay cutty gripped firmly in her hand. It was buried with her in a pauper's grave in Alyth cemetery where my mother's entire family is buried.

★

When my mother was six, she learned her first song, 'The Twa Brothers'. My Uncle Donald, my mother's brother, knew all the songs from his father, and because my mother had two brothers, they decided that would be her first song.

Around the same time, my granny decided to send my mother to school so that she would be able to read the letters coming home from the family during the war. She was at school for nine months and learned to read a bit. Then she left and didn't go back.

One day, she came running home and burst through the door shouting, 'Mammy, you better come down to the Connies – something has happened!' The Connies were a row of houses where travellers stayed in Rattray. Her mother wrapped the shawl around her shoulders and followed her down the road. When they got there the police were in one of the houses.

'What's happened, Jean?' my granny said to the woman who was being questioned.

'Oh, that mother of mine has killed her granddaughter because she was playing truant from school.'

That day, the grandmother had found out that she wasn't at

school when the education inspector came to her house looking
for the girl. When the girl came home, the granny started to beat
her and wouldn't stop, and killed her. She got away with it – the
police called it a tinkers' squabble, but her family made her an
outcast and never talked to her again.

*

In the summer of 1913, my granny, her sons and my mother
were camped up at Cortachy pearl-fishing. They lived on a piece
of ground that belonged to Lord Ogilvie of Airlie Castle. They
had a horse and cart and used to go hawking in Glen Clova. One
day on their way home to the camp, my granny and my mother
were walking and my mother's brother Andy was riding on the
front of the cart. Suddenly there was an awful noise behind
them, and a small sports car flew past. (It was the first car my
mother had ever seen.) Well, the horse took fright and bolted,
Andy was thrown off, and the cart wheel went over his leg. The
car stopped and Lord Ogilvie jumped out. There was a young
lady with him, and she attended to the cuts on Andy's leg and
wiped the blood off with her hanky. Lord Ogilvie was so upset,
and wanted to take Andy in his car to the doctor at Kirriemuir,
but my granny wouldn't hear word of it. So Lord Ogilvie helped
him back to the camp, and then he said to my mother, 'I have to
go away tomorrow, but could you please call at the house, and let
my mother know how the boy is?'

So the next day my granny took my mother with her to the
castle. Granny rang the bell, and they had to wait a long time
before anyone answered the door. Eventually a servant appeared,
my granny explained what happened and they were told to wait
outside. A few minutes later they were taken into the castle and
asked to wait in the front hall. Then down the stairs came the
dowager duchess. My mother was so surprised by the rustle of
her dress as she came down the stairs that she couldn't speak and
just stared. The duchess took them into a side room, pressed the
bell for the butler, and ordered tea and biscuits for them. My
mother was fascinated by the pictures on the wall, all of them oil

paintings. She didn't pay much attention to what her mother and the duchess were talking about. The duchess greatly admired my mother's curly hair. While they were having their tea, the lady excused herself and left them alone for a while. Soon, my mother heard that wonderful noise of the rustle of the lady's dress again, and in she came with a big box of ribbons saying, 'These ribbons will do your hair, my child.' Then she gave her half a crown and gave my granny an envelope, saying it was from her Lord Ogilvie. They were just about to leave when the lady said, 'Go round the back and I will have a word with the cook to give you some food.' They were given two tablecloths full of all kinds of food from the cook, and they were a happy family that night, I can tell you. My granny waited till she got back to the camp before she opened the envelope. There was one pound in it, which was a lot of money in those days.

*

My mother was eight years old when the 1914 war broke out. Her brother Donald and her uncle Jimmy Jack joined the Scottish Rifles in 1915. They were sworn in by an old man called Mr Spalding from Blairgowrie who was the recruiting officer then.

They were only six months in the Scottish Rifles before they came home and then deserted. They cleared off to the Highlands and travelled all over the north. They stayed a few weeks at Inverness, but of course they had my granny, my mother and Andy with them, and were to afraid to stay any longer. There were too many travellers there who knew them, and they were afraid they would tell on them. So they moved to Alloa. They got a house there, and my mother went to school. My granny Martha and her brother Jimmy Jack worked on a farm, Donald got a job on the railway, and my mother's brother Andy worked in a glass factory blowing bottles. Donald was terrified they would get caught for desertion. One night the family went to a show in Alloa's town hall, but Donald didn't go. They were about an hour in the hall when he came in and said, 'Come on Jimmy, I'm going away. I can't stay here any longer.' So they all left the hall and packed up, and next morning they got the train to Dundee.

As they arrived at the station in Dundee, a funny thing happened. There was a battalion of soldiers standing on the platform. Donald looked at them and saw an officer who was in charge. He jumped out of the train and went over and spoke to him, and there and then Donald and Jimmy were arrested. They asked for a transfer from the Scottish Rifles to the Black Watch. Both of them were drafted to France.

Donald was severely wounded at Givenchy at the battle of the Somme in 1916. He was sent home to recuperate and Jimmy was given leave to go with him. My granny nursed him better, but there was no way he wanted to go back to the army. They had a wee house in Dundee at the time, where they stayed, and, once more, they became deserters, on the hide again.

They all went to the pictures one night, and halfway through the film, my uncle Donald got a tap on the shoulder – it was the military police. He and Jimmy were arrested for the second time. My granny and my mother were so upset. They found out later it was a traveller woman who had shopped on them – she had known they were going to the pictures that night.

Next day, they were told they were to join their regiment to go back to the Somme. When they got to the Dundee station, my mother's brother Donald put his three middle fingers in the hinge of the train door, and told Jimmy to close it hard. Jimmy didn't realise his hand was in the door, and what a shock he got. The three fingers were cut off.

Well, that was Donald's army career over, but not Jimmy's. He had to go away by himself on the train. Donald was only left with a thumb and a pinkie, but it never held him back in any way. He couldn't read or write, so that didn't matter, but everything else he did perfectly. He could always count his money; that was no problem for him.

Jimmy Jack stayed in the army until his two years were up, and he came home safe and sound, thank God. The men never told the family anything they had been through in the war. They kept that a secret and they went to their graves with this secret. I think perhaps they just didn't want to relive that awful time in their lives.

★

My granny's favourite glen was Glen Isla. She hawked there all the time, selling her wares out of her basket. She and my mother went up there one day just before Christmas, when my mother was about ten years old. Glen Isla was great at Christmas time. All the folk in the glen knew my granny so well and they called her the newspaper, because she told them all the news from Blairgowrie and Alyth. She and my mother went up there at least once a month. This Christmas in particular they went to a wee cotter hoose. The folk that had lived there before had moved, and there was a new family.

My granny approached the door and knocked. A woman came out with a scowl on her face. 'What do you tinkers want at my door?'

My granny said, 'We have come to see if you need anything out of my basket today.'

'Get you away from my door, or I will set the dog on you. And don't come back.'

So they moved on to the next farm, which McKenzie owned. My granny told Mr McKenzie what had happened, 'What?' he said. 'Did you no ken they are travellers themselves? Stewarts, they are.' My granny was stunned to hear this news, and she said she would go back in on her way down the glen. They arrived there an hour later, and knocked on the door.

'Well,' said my granny when the woman opened the door, 'What are you up to?'

The woman replied, 'I married a non-traveller and I don't want the folk of the glen knowing this.'

'But they already ken,' said my granny. 'Who are you anyway?'

'Well, my name is Martha Stewart,' said the woman.

'What? That's my name! Where did you come fae?'

'Inverness,' she replied.

'Oh, you're the Stewarts fae Inverness. I ken a lot o them –

nice folk they are. They come tae the berry pickin every year.'

Just then a wee lassie came past her mother at the door. She was covered in scabs from impetigo.

'How many weans have you got?' asked my granny.

'Four,' said the woman, 'and they all have the scab.'

'My good God Almighty,' said my granny, 'what have you got to put on them?'

'Nothing,' said the woman. 'Away up here in this glen and no near a shop, I am just letting it take its toll till it gets better.'

'Have you no heard of Lucy Arnots?' my granny asked.

'What's that?'

'It's a nut that you dig up from a certain plant, and it cures it. Come wi me,' said my granny, and they went out into the garden to dig for them. My granny got about two dozen, and crushed them up to a pulp. 'Now dab it on all their scabs, for about a week, and they will soon disappear.'

The woman thanked my granny, and she and my mother left the glen to go back to Blairgowrie. A month later they were in the glen again, and went to the woman's door.

'How are you all today?' my granny asked.

'Thank you for the Christmas present you gave me,' the woman said.

'What? I never gave you a present.'

'Oh yes you did,' said the woman. She shouted inside. 'Come here, bairns,' and they all came out with clear faces clear as a baby's bum. All the scabs had gone.

*

My mother was growing into a real beauty. All the travellers said, 'Aye Martha, she will turn a few heads, that one.' By this time, with Donald and Andy working, they had enough money saved to buy a house in Rattray at Rattray Cross. This gave my granny a great independence that she had never felt before. Instead of getting a dog to keep away intruders, she got a kea laddie, a jackdaw they had got from this old man who came to the door one day. They kept it in the garden on a long rope and anyone coming to the door left with blood running out of their ankles. He was a fierce bird, was John – that's what they called him. The bird lived for a few years, then a cat caught and ate it. We found the carcass outside one morning.

At that time, my mother played a lot with her cousin Andy MacGregor. He was a jewel of a boy and was the most sensible person you could meet, but he had a speech impediment, what the travellers called a thrummelbore – he had no roof in his mouth. He was the only one who could go up to the kea laddie without being attacked. It never pecked him once. He was the one who put it in the shed at night, took it out in the morning and tied it up again. Later, Andy died from tuberculosis. It was a great loss to our family when he passed away and my mother mourned him for years.

★

My mother was now seventeen years old, and wasn't short of admirers. Her first boyfriend was from Blair. He asked her out and she went, wondering all the time what her mother and brothers would think. But she also had a strong will of her own and if she wanted to do something, nobody could stop her. Well, she and the boy went for a walk and when he took her back home, they stopped in a close not far from the house. Her brother Donald was sent to look for her, and, by God, he found her kissing this boy. He grabbed him by the scruff of the neck, and kicked his arse all down the road. What he said to my mother when he got her home she wouldn't tell me, but I bet she got an earful.

During this time, Donald, Andy and Jimmy Jack were getting ready to go to Ireland to do some pearl-fishing. They asked my granny if they could take my mother with them because she would be able to read all the signs of places for them. My granny agreed to let her go only if they kept a close eye on her. So they said they would.

This is when my mother met my father. She had known him when they were younger, but hadn't seen him for many years.

His mother and her mother were full cousins. The mother of one of my grannies was my other granny's aunt. I'd better stop there because it gets a bit complicated. Anyway, my mother and father were second cousins. My father's name was Alex, and although it was always spelled with an 'x', it was pronounced by everyone as 'Alec'.

The four of them arrived in Ireland, and went to camp at the Black Water, beside my father's parents, Jock and Nancy. They were also pearl-fishers. They all had something to eat, then they sat round the fire, telling all the news from Scotland and generally catching up on family gossip.

Next morning, the men went pearl-fishing. My mother was left at the camp with the rest of the girls, tidying up and cooking their breakfast. My granny (my father's mother Nancy) put a huge pot full of water on the outside fire. 'What's that for?' my mother asked.

'It's for the eggs for the breakfast.' Then my granny started piling the eggs into the pot. My mothers' two eyes were on stalks watching the amount of eggs going in.

'How many did you put in there?' asked my mother.

'Six dozen. I hope that will be enough the day cause that's all I have left till I get to the shop.' The men came home an hour later and the eggs were boiling all that time. When they arrived, my granny spread out a pure white tablecloth, and put all the eggs from the pot in the middle of the table with two loaves of bread and butter. They all sat round and tucked into the eggs. My father ate a dozen.

Everything was cleared away when they were finished, and the men went back to pearl-fishing. My grandfather Jock found a wonderful pearl that day. He went to the chemist to have it weighed. That's were they took the pearls because it was the only shop that dealt in grains. The pearl weighed forty grains exactly. My grandfather sold it to the chemist for twenty pounds. The chemist wasn't allowed to keep it – it had to go to the crown – but he was compensated for it.

The family then moved to a small village called Swanlinbar. My mother stayed in Ireland for a few weeks then, and they got a good few pearls. When she returned home with her brothers, they sold them to Cairncross the Jewellers in Perth, which is where they took all the pearls they found.

★

That Hogmanay, they had a fantastic time. A lot of travellers came first-footing them and so there was a great ceilidh. One of the young men there kept looking and looking at my mother and he seemed very interested in her. She got so embarrassed with him that she went through to the kitchen and shouted for him to follow. He was delighted that she had taken notice of him, so he swaggered through to the kitchen with a glint in his eye.

She didn't want a repeat of the last time Donald had caught her with a boy. Donald and Andy were too busy drinking and singing to notice the young traveller eyeing her, so she decided to take the matter into her own hands and sort it out before there was a rumble. 'What do you think you're doing?' she asked. 'You haven't taken your eyes off me all night. What are you playing at?'

She took him to the back door and pushed him out and warned him not to come back, or she would tell her brothers about him pestering her. So off he went like a mad March hare and never returned. When he next saw her in town, he turned his head away. 'Thank God,' she said to herself, 'he has got the message.'

★

The next year, my uncles went again to Ireland to pearl-fish, and my mother returned with them. Again they stayed beside my grandparents, Jock and Nancy. When they arrived, the girls took my mother aside and told her my father fancied her. He had asked them to tell her as he was too shy to do so himself. At tea that night, sitting round the outside fire, she kept glancing over at him. He didn't look in her direction all night, so this gave her a chance to study him. She liked what she saw, but kept it to herself and she never even mentioned it to the girls later on.

The next day, she went with the girls with my granny Nancy to do the shopping. When they got to the town they went to the butcher's first, and my granny Nancy bought three pounds of bacon, six oxtails, and six pigs' ears. My mother was amazed – she never knew before that folk ate them. When they got back to the camp, the fire was put on and the big pots brought out. My granny put the oxtails into one pot, and in another she put the pigs' ears. Again, my mother couldn't believe it. All the girls helped to peel a mountain of potatoes. When the men came back the food was all ready. They sat round the tablecloth where the potatoes were emptied out in the middle, and plates of oxtails and pigs' lugs arrived. My mother watched to see what her brothers' reaction to the meal would be, but they ate up heartily, with no comment. My mother wasn't eating and her brother Donald asked her why. 'I am no eatin foxes' tails,' she said.

The whole camp broke out in laughter. 'That's no foxes' tails, it's oxtails,' her brother Donald said.

'I don't care if its rats' tails, I am not eating it!' So she settled for potatoes that night.

The next morning, the girls were going out drookerin – reading palms. My mother had never done this before, but she went with them to see what it was like. They went from house to house and they got a good lot of money, but my mother never took to it at all.

★

They arrived back in Scotland just as the harvest was about to start. There was a job waiting for them with the same farmer they worked for every year. That year there was also another travelling family to help with the harvest. An unfortunate thing happened to my mother's cousin, who was named Donald, that year. They were cutting corn and he was late getting back after piece-time. He was running across the field to get back to work and he happened to run past just as a scythe came down, cutting his shin. The farmer's wife washed and bandaged it, but bone disease soon set in and he died.

It wasn't a very pleasant time for the family then; the ceilidh round the fire just didn't happen that year. Then the sister of the woman of the other family working there died. The woman asked my granny Martha to look after the children while they went down to the funeral at Kirriemuir. My granny agreed, and the next day the man and woman headed away to the funeral. They were to be back the day after the funeral, but they didn't return. It was a week before they finally got back. They said they had got involved with their family and been on a drinking spree. Then the man started fighting with her brother and was arrested and spent two days in jail. He had a cut above his eye and the other eye was black. 'Serves you right,' said my granny. 'Don't you know it is unlucky to fight at a funeral? But you thickened bobambies wouldn't ken that.' She went on and on at the two of them, and they just sat there with there heads hung low, never uttering a word. After she had her say, she fed them and made tea. All was fine again.

★

Early in 1925, Jock, Nancy and my father came over for a few days to visit. When they arrived at the house, my mother scurried into the kitchen. 'Belle,' shouted her mother, 'put the kettle on for a drop o tea till the soup's ready.'

My mother was very nervous about coming through to the living room, because she knew my father was there. Slowly walking in with the cups of tea, she held her head down. She remembered what his sisters had said about him fancying her. She said hello to them all and cuddled Nancy and Jock. My father said, 'What about me?'

'I don't cuddle strange boys.'

'Ah well,' my father said. 'It's you that's missing out.' She blushed shyly and left the room.

Two days later, the visitors left to go back to Ireland. Donald and Jimmy said they would be over in the summer as usual, to pearl-fish. In the middle of July 1925 they headed back to Ireland, and my mother went with them again. Jock and Nancy were so pleased to see them. The first night the older ones had a drink round the fire, and Donald asked my mother to sing a song. She was mortified, but she knew they knew she could sing. She sang an Irish song for them: 'If I Was a Blackbird', one of Donald's favourites. There wasn't a dry eye between the older ones, although my mother told the girls she thought it was the drink that made them so emotional.

Then my father came up to my mother and asked her to go a walk with him, and she went. Hearing the sniggering of the rest of the girls, she blushed. They walked down the side of the river chatting away. My father told her it was the first time he had heard her sing and that he liked it.

A few days later, he asked my mother to go with him to a farm about two miles away. He said he had something to show her. So off they went to Mr Hennessey's farm and when they got there, he took her around the back of the steading and showed her a newly built bow-topped wagon.

'Well, what do you think of it?' he asked her.

'It's lovely,' my mother said.

'Well,' said my father, 'it's yours if you marry me. I was all winter building it for us.'

My mother was so shocked she choked. 'You mean you're asking me to marry you?'

'Yes,' said my father, 'why not?'

My father was never a romantic man and that is how he proposed to my mother. So, on 17 August 1925, they were married in the church at Ballymony in Ireland. Why, I don't know, but my mother got married in black. We travellers would say that was very unlucky, as indeed would the non-traveller.

My father was a great player of the bagpipes, and he made his money playing at fairs and busking in the streets. The two of them settled into life in the bow top, but there was one problem. They hadn't told my mother's mother back in Scotland that they were getting married. My mother knew she wouldn't approve because they were second cousins. 'Too sib a freen', she would say.

My father's sister Jeannie tried to teach my mother drookerin but she refused to do it, so my father was the sole breadwinner. That didn't please his family, because they believed women should pull their own weight.

Eventually, when the pearl season was over, they had to return to Scotland. They all headed back, ready to face the fireworks and the wrath of my granny.

Well, they arrived in Blairgowrie a few days later. My granny Martha wasn't in when they got to the house, but she always left the key in the roan pipe, so they were able to get into the house.

My granny Martha was an argumentative woman who had to get her own way in everything, and she ruled the roost. She could 'clip cloots wi her tongue'. This is an old travellers' saying about a sharp- and long-tongued person, and she sure was that. So can you imagine how my mother and father felt in facing her? She came home half an hour later and walked in with her groceries, glad to see her bairns. Then she saw my father.

'What's he doin here?' she asked, and turned to Donald. He said nothing. Then she turned to Jimmy, who looked away. Finally, she looked at my mother. 'Well, lassie, are you going to answer me?' My mother looked at her and swallowed hard.

'Well, mother,' she said, 'this is my man.'

'What do you mean, your man?' asked my granny.

'We are married and there's nothing you or anybody can do about it.'

Well, flames came out of my granny's mouth at this point. She was spitting and tongue-tied. She sat down in a chair, and went quiet for a minute.

'By the Lord God above, lassie, what have you done? Do you no ken he's too sib a freen to you? Your weans will be all deformed.'

My mother and father sat quietly. My mother knew it was best to let her get it all out, and then all would eventually be accepted. How wrong she was. My father had to sleep in the shed that night.

'You are no sleeping under the same roof as my daughter, man or no man. I would be happy if you two would move out in the morning. I don't care where you go, just get out of my house.'

'A wicked old woman,' my father said.

*

Well, my mother and father moved back to Ireland to his folk, where they were made welcome. 'Aye,' said my father's mother, 'she always had a wicked temper, my cousin Mattie, but stay away for a while, and she'll calm down. That's what happens when you have no man to control you. I told you to let her know about the wedding beforehand.'

'Oh no,' said my mother, 'she would have stopped it.'

My mother stayed in Ireland for a few weeks. Then she found out she was expecting a baby, and wanted to go home to her family in Scotland.

'Well, you can go if you like Belle, but I am staying here,' said my father.

My mother had to ask Donald to send her the fare home, because my father refused to give her any money. She picked up the money at the post office three days later, and headed back to Scotland. She arrived safely, and even her mother welcomed her home, probably because my father wasn't with her. Her mother didn't lecture her any more that time, because she had been well warned by Donald and Andy, and also because of my mother's condition.

Months later she had a wee boy, my brother John. He was the apple of my granny's eye, and Donald, Andy and Jimmy worshipped him too.

Several months later, my father came to Blairgowrie to see his son, and stayed for a few days. 'Belle,' he said to my mother, 'are you coming home with me?'

'Alright, I will,' she said.

Her mother heard her and stepped into the kitchen where they were. 'Well,' she said, 'you two can go, but you're no taking John.' No matter how they pleaded and argued she wouldn't give in. So my mother and father left John with my granny, Donald, Andy and Jimmy. My mother stayed away for about six months this time, but longed to get back to see John. She had a big argument with my father, and ended up returning to Scotland, where she stayed for a year. My father never got in touch with her at all, not even to ask for the baby, but Granny Nancy did. She wrote to my mother often, as did his sister Jeannie. They said he was a very stubborn man. After a year, my mother went back to my father in Ireland.

They travelled for a while with my father's family, but like most mother- and daughter-in-laws, Nancy and my mother just couldn't agree. So my mother and father were mostly on their own. One day my father was in the river pearl-fishing at Ballyshannon with only his trousers on. (But before I tell you about this incident I must point out that although my family of travellers were not church goers, we have our own very strong faith.) When he had finished fishing, he lit a fire to dry himself. That night, though, he took very ill and had a high fever. They sent for the doctor, who he said he had inflammation of the bowels. So they took him to Ballyshannon hospital where the nurses were all nuns. He sank into a coma for seven days and he was on the danger list. His family were allowed to visit him at any time. My mother and the rest of the family lived two miles from the hospital. My granny and my mother would walk to the hospital twice a day to visit him. One day the doctor told them to go home and return with the whole family, because he was in a deeper coma and they thought he wouldn't last the night. So my mother stayed with my father while my granny hurried home to fetch the rest of the family. On her way to tell them, she had to pass a small row of cottages and standing at one of the doors was an old woman. She said to my granny, 'Excuse me, daughter, but have you anyone ill in hospital? I watch you pass so often going up there.'

'Oh dear, aye', said my granny. 'My son's up there, and they say he won't see morning, so I am going home to fetch his father and the rest of the family to come and see him.'

'Are you sure, daughter, they can do no more for him up there?'

'Oh no,' said my granny, 'they have done all they can. He is in a deep coma, and the doctor said it is only a matter of time.' She was crying hard by this time.

'Well,' said the old woman, 'are you a believer in God?'

'Oh yes,' my granny said. 'Who can we lippin on but God?'

Then the old woman said, 'Just wait a minute till I get my shawl, and I will take you to St Patrick's well. It's only up the road a bit. If it doesn't cure him, it'll certainly not kill him, for it's only God's pure holy water.'

So the old woman took a bottle with her and they both went up to the well. Instead of going back to tell his father and family, my granny made her way back to the hospital. By this time my father was in a small side ward, with my mother holding his hand. My granny got an awful fright when she saw him because she thought he was dead already, but he wasn't. Of course, she had to get the permission from the doctor to give him the holy water. The doctor said it was alright, but the nurse wasn't allowed to give it to him – my granny had to do it herself. So she wet her fingers and rubbed it over his lips, but he made no attempt to swallow, or open his lips at all.

So instead she opened his lips and poured a small amount into his mouth, and he swallowed it. She did it again twice. Then she told the nurse, who was delighted. So she hurried home to tell his father and the family. She told them all that had happened. My mother was still in the hospital with him. That night they all went to see him, but there was no change in him. They sat with him for a few hours, then went home, and so did my mother.

The next morning when they all arrived at the hospital, he was back in the big ward, and had eaten all his breakfast. He was sitting up smiling at them. Oh, now the hospital was in an uproar about the holy water, and on the placards at the shop it said, 'ST PATRICK'S HOLY WATER CURES TINKER BOY'. It was all over the newspapers as well. Two days later, my father was allowed home. To this day, Ireland is a very special country for my family, and my father was a very special man.

★

Even in those days, travellers were told by the police to move on. The day my sister Cathie was born in Strabane County Tyrone, 2 November 1927, the police came to move them on. My father's sister Jeannie had just delivered Cathie.

'You must move on,' said the guards. My father was away busking in the town. Jeannie explained to the men that my mother had just given birth, but they wouldn't believe her, and refused to look in the caravan to see. They were just being awkward. Jeannie ran to her sister's caravan, and asked her brother-in-law to explain it to the police. He made them look inside, and they could see the baby was newly born. It was impossible for my mother and father to move anyway, because the horse had gone into the bog the night before, and had to be shot by the police, so they hadn't a horse to pull the caravan. The police wouldn't take no for an answer, but gave them twenty-four hours before they had to move.

The next day, my father had to go between the shafts and pull the caravan himself, with my mother and the baby sitting on the front. He pulled it ten miles to where his sister was staying with her caravan. When they wanted to move after that, my father's brother-in-law, Donald Higgins, would move his own caravan first with his horse, then he would come back for my mother and father's.

*

One afternoon, my father and Donald Higgins went to the shops for something for tea. Now, Donald was a cheery man, always laughing. On their way home, they were walking in a field which had a track road running parallel to it. 'I wonder what time it is, Donald,' my father said.

'We can ask this man comin doon the road.'

As the man approached, my father asked him the time. There was no answer. 'Maybe', said my father 'he is deaf.' So as the man passed on about five yards, my father shouted after him, 'Hi min! What time is it?'

The man turned and said in a deep voice, 'If you meet me

halfway, I will tell you the time.' Well, my father turned to Donald. 'Run, Donald!' he shouted. It was nearly dark by this time now, they couldn't see clearly where they were going and the fear was in them. Donald was running like hell behind my father, and a few yards across from him. They came to a fence at the end of the field and my father shouted, 'Jump, Donald! Jump!' My father hopped over safe enough, but all he heard from Donald was a fading 'Aaaaaaaaaaaaaaa!' He had jumped into a quarry, and fallen right to the bottom. He was alright, although he had a lot of bumps and bruises for a while. They never went through that field again.

A few days later, my mother was in the caravan by herself, as my father was away busking. Cathie was lying asleep on the bed. All was quiet. My mother looked over to the bed where Cathie was asleep, and the blanket moved off Cathie's shoulders and folded itself down to her feet, as neat as anything. My mother wasn't frightened because my family believed in warnings, and she knew there was some thing wrong back home. She got in touch with her family and was told that her cousin in Perth, who they called Jimmy the Bird, had died from tuberculosis. So she and my father decided to go home for the funeral. My father wasn't too excited about it, because it would mean facing my granny Martha, but at least he would be able to see his son John, who was two by then.

After the funeral, my father went back to Ireland, and left my mother in Scotland with Cathie and John. She stayed for a week, then returned to Ireland again, leaving John, of course, with my granny Martha.

*

My mother fell pregnant again, so my mother and father came home to Scotland to have the child there, but all was not well. My granny Martha was to blame, with her interference in everything. On 8 June 1929, my mother gave birth to my brother Andy, at home, of course. The day after the birth, she woke up in the morning, and my granny gave her a cup of tea.

She went to drink it and spilled the tea on the bed. When my granny looked at her, she saw my mother's mouth was all twisted to the side of her face. My granny sent for the doctor, who examined her and diagnosed her with Bell's Palsy. My father, who was very annoyed by this time with my granny, took it out on my mother, saying, 'No man could stand looking at a twisted faced woman like her. I am off, and I won't be back. Keep her.'

My father left that day and didn't come back for many years. When my mother was up and about again she wouldn't go out the door with the Bell's Palsy. A cousin of hers came to see her one day and said she had a cure. 'Get a bottle of olive oil, keep it beside the fire to keep warm, and rub it on your face three times a day. Don't wash your hair, and keep a headscarf on.' Well, my mother did this for six months. One day she woke up, and her face was back to normal. The first thing she did was to wash her hair. What a relief that was.

My mother had not heard from my father all this time, not even to ask about the children. My mother now had three of them to look after – John, Andy and Cathie – so she said to her mother, 'I must get a job.' She took the charabanc to Dundee and started work in Keillers jam factory. The hours were long, but she managed to do it for a good while, until the boyfriend of one of the girls started chatting up my mother and the girlfriend became terribly jealous.

'Awa you go, I'm not interested in your man,' my mother told her. But later on that day, the girl tipped some boiling jam over my mother's leg and that was the end of the jam factory. My mother went through great pain for a long time with her leg. It took three months to heal fully.

★

When the traveller men knew my mother was away from my father, they paid unexpected visits to her brothers, but it was really her they came to see. I remember an old traveller man saying to me one day, 'You ken Sheila, your mother was the best-looking woman among the travellers in Perthshire,' and I believe she was.

One day there was a knock at my granny's door. It was one of the travellers who stayed in a wee house in Rattray. My granny opened the door and let her in. She was in some state.

'My wee lassie Maggie has run awa with a man.'

'God bless my soul,' said my granny Martha. 'Who is this laddie?'

'Ah, but I didn't say laddie Mattie, I said a man.'

'Sit doon here,' my granny said, pointing to a chair in the corner. 'Belle, put the cacavie on for some weed. The poor creature is shakin.'

My mother made her a cup of tea and sat down to see what she had to say. 'I wouldna care,' said the old woman, wringing her hands together with a tear in her eye, 'but he is a married man with twa bairns. Now, is that no shaming? And her only sixteen.'

My granny put her arm around her. 'Never mind, Mary, all will be fine in the morning.'

'No it won't, because his wife is chappin at my door looking for him. What am I tae dae Mattie?'

'I'll come wi you and see if she's awa noo,' said my granny.

So both of them went round to her wee house, but before they reached it, they could hear her shouting like a bull. 'Come oot, you bloody twisted whore and gie me my man back.'

My granny went up to her and said, 'What's wrong, Jeannie? Have ye lost your senses, woman? There's nae man worth aa this carry-on.'

'Did you hear what that silly wee bitch did, Matty? Stole my man.'

'Aye,' said my granny, 'now it will be her getting aa the beatings you got for a good pockle of years, and she will be the one skivvying tae him and hawking for his money to go to the pub wi. Aye, you must be sorry tae lose such a man. God help you.'

All went quiet for a while. Jeannie was thinking over what my granny had said. Then she let out a big howl o laughter, till the tears ran doon her face. 'Aye, Mattie, I am well rid o him, God help her noo. Come on into the hoose and get a cup of tea, or maybe something a wee bit stronger.'

My granny liked a wee tipple as well as the next yin.

★

My mother went to the shop one day and walked past a squad of Irishmen digging up the road. They all whistled at my mother except one, but he couldn't keep his eyes off her, and she noticed him too. Returning from the shop, she was carrying a big bag of groceries and when she got to where the men were, the one that had noticed carried all her bags to the house. She was very attracted to him and she sensed he was attracted to her as well. They chatted for a while and he told her his name was Jimmy Veesy. He asked to see her that night, but she refused. Instead she said that she could meet him the following night. 'That's fine,' he said, 'tomorrow will be great.' Then he left her at the door and she went inside.

They started going out together pretty regularly and soon fell madly in love. After about a year, she became pregnant to him but had a miscarriage. Her mother wasn't too happy, because, after all, my mother was still married. So my mother once more took the wrath of her tongue, but she wouldn't stop seeing him because their love was too deep. When the road work was over, Jimmy Veesy moved away to Dundee, but they carried on meeting up.

One day, there was a knock on the door and my mother answered. It was my father's mother. My granny Martha had written her a letter, telling her all about Jimmy and she had come straight over from Ireland to try to sort out this mess. In those days, the mother of a family was the boss, and the children had to do what they were told. The two grannies decided that my mother and father must get back together. So my father's mother went back to Ireland to tell my father he had to go back to his wife and bairns.

It had been five years since my mother and father had split up, but my granny Martha put her foot down too; my mother had to go back to her husband. A few weeks later, my father and his mother arrived at the door. The two grannies had it out with my parents and forced them to get back together. So my father stayed and lived with my mother, the children and my granny Martha.

★

Sheila Stewart

Owre yon Hill

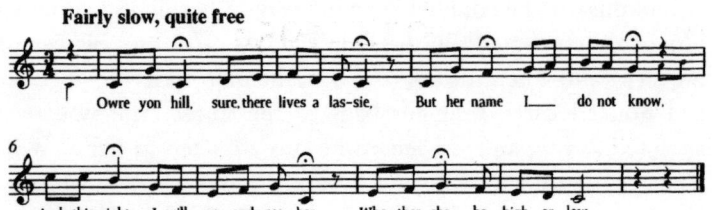

Owre yon hill, sure, there lives a lassie,
But her name I do not know,
And this night I will go and see her,
Whether she be high, or low.

'Lassie I have come to see you,
But perhaps it is in vain,
But if you will kindly entertain me
Maybe I'll call back again.

'Lassie I have got gold and silver,
Lassie I have got diamond stones,
Lassie I have got ships on the ocean,
They will be yours, love, if you'll be mine.'

'What care I for your gold and silver,
What care I for your diamond stones,
And what care I for your ships on the ocean?
All I want is a fine young man.'

1934–1954

My mother fell pregnant for the fourth time. She was carrying me. All was fine for a while, but there were still arguments in the home between my granny and my father. My mother and father had no money to get a house of their own, so they depended on staying with her. Two days before I was born, she threw them out of the house and they had nowhere to go. My mother was due her baby any time so my father was panicking. He went to the man who owned the Angus Hotel in Blairgowrie because he knew him very well and the man had property all over the town.

'Well,' he said to my father, 'I've only got one place where you can go: the stable behind the hotel – a few weeks ago I sold all my horses. You can put a curtain up or something and corner off a part of it for yourselves.'

Two days later, on 7 July 1935, I was born. I weighed two and a half pounds. The nurse thought I was a twin because I was so small, but no, I was one of a kind. The nurse brought dolls' clothes to put on me, but my mother had to take them in because I was so tiny.

My mother, father, Andy, Cathie and myself left there a week later and got a hut at Blacklaw, where they picked berries. They saved up that berry season and began to rent a house from Hill Whitson of Rattray at two and six a week. Now that they were in their own house, my granny accepted them again. She said, 'It's about time, Alex, youse two stood on your ain twa feet, and made a hame for your bairns.' My mother just had to try to be content because she had lost Jimmy Veesy.

★

In 1939, my granny Martha died. I was four years old at the time. Although I wasn't allowed to go to the funeral, I watched it pass at Rattray Cross with my mother's cousin Andy. I remember it like yesterday. Solicitors, doctors and many high-class people from Blairgowrie attended. I remember the hearse passing me. All the shops in the high street drew their blinds as the funeral procession went by. My granny Martha had been well-respected in Blair. She was buried in Alyth next to her husband Dan. It was a day of gloom which I'll never forget – I knew things would never be the same.

My mother retreated into herself. All she did was lie in bed every day, mourning her mother. The cousins and aunties of the family rallied around to look after us children while my mother was depressed. It took her a week to finally get out of bed, and things slowly got back to normal, but it was a long, long time before she got over the death of my granny, although my mother and father got on a lot better without her mother's interference.

★

My mother and father's house at that time was up the Park Hill road, next to an old drovers' inn. This was too close for comfort for my mother, with my father drinking, but their names were down with the local council for a house, and we were then given one at 51 MacDonald Crescent. It was very close to the flax factory and my father began working there.

One day, my mother and father were up the town when, in the Well Meadow, they saw a man, a woman and a wee girl sitting on the grass. The woman was crying. My parents went over and spoke to them. The man was a Canadian and said his name was Ace Mitchell. The woman, Mickey, was his wife and the child, Marlene, was their daughter. They had nowhere to live, and although my mother and father had four children, they said they could stay with us.

We only had two bedrooms in the house, so us kids were put into one, while Ace Mitchell, his wife and daughter were put into the other. Ace was very fond of piping and my father taught him to play. When conscription came, my father and Ace joined the Black Watch as pipers and were sent to Dunkirk. Pipers in these days were also stretcher-bearers; they took the wounded off the field and back to the Red Cross camp.

Their captain was a man from Blairgowrie. One day, my father was at the battlefield when the captain got wounded in the leg. There were no stretchers at this time, so my father lifted him on his shoulder and carried him back to the Red Cross camp. When they reached the camp, he laid his captain on a bed. He stared up at my father and said, 'Is that you, Stewart? Did you just save me from the battlefield?'

My father answered, 'Yes, I did.'

'Well, if I had known it was a tink that saved me, I would've told you to leave me to die.'

That was the thanks my father got for saving his life. Until the day my father died, he never forgot what the captain had said to him. I won't tell you the captain's name because it was so long ago now and it's best forgotten about.

My father's regiment was told to disperse as the Germans were near at hand. His platoon kept together and ran for many miles until they came to a deserted farmhouse that had been taken over by the Germans and had then been deserted. My father's platoon discovered a cellar full of wine, so of course they stayed for a long time. I think they drank all the wine in the cellar. Later on after he came home, my mother asked him about this, and he just smiled with a twinkle in his eye.

During the time my father was hiding in the farmhouse, my mother got no letters from him at all, and she thought it was because they were holding letters back from her. My father had been writing to my mother in our Cant language and the army had had experts in to try and decipher it, but they couldn't make it out. My father had been sent for and was told by the captain to stop writing it in this language. One letter she had received was sent all stroked out and the only thing she could make out was 'Love, Alex'.

One day, the sun was shining and all our neighbours were sitting on their doorsteps. When my mother saw the postman coming down the road she shouted to him without thinking, 'Hi postie! Any French letters for me the day?' She wondered what the neighbours were laughing at. Then she realised what she had said and ran mortified into the house. She wasn't seen again that day.

The next time my mother got word was when she received a telegram from the war office to say my father had been killed and was now buried with his pipes. There was a great sadness then and my mother cried for days on end. It was a good job she had Mickey Mitchell for company. She consoled my mother a lot, and gave her strength.

A few months later, my brother Andy went off to school one morning and came running back very excited. 'Mammy, Mammy,' he shouted, 'my daddy is comin doon the road!'

'Awa, ye silly laddie, how could he?' my mother said, but she ran out to see and sure enough it was my father, the worst for wear but alive, thank God. He explained the story about hiding up in an empty farmhouse and drinking it dry. Well, my mother made a dive at him and when my mother started she was as bad as my granny Martha. She too could could clip cloots wi her tongue.

My father had been hoping for a party to celebrate his home-coming, but my mother had other ideas – she was too angry with him. He didn't get his party until Hogmanay. My father had been separated from Ace Mitchell, and couldn't tell Mickey any news of him at all, but a few weeks later Ace came home safe and sound. Everyone was happy now. My mother fell pregnant again, and she seemed so cheerful. She went about like a clucking hen. She taught me my first song, 'Twa Heeds are Better than Yin', and she took me up to my uncle Donald so I could sing it to him. He gave me half a crown and said I was ready to start some serious learning of the ballads. I often went to stay with him after that and he began teaching me them.

*

One day, my mother brought home another homeless couple

named Ivor and Annie. They were poor creatures and they had a few slates missing up top. My father pitched a tent for them in our back garden, where they were quite content. We always used to play games at night to amuse ourselves – we had no television, only a radio that needed an accumulator, which needed to be charged often and never was. One night, my father said to Cathie, 'Go and tell Ivor and Annie to come in and join in wir games. They must be lonely oot in that tent all the time.'

So in they came. Ace, Mickey and Marlene were still there as well. My mother made us all tea and we played Tricks – we had to see who could stand on one leg for the longest or who could go the longest without speaking . . . You can guarantee my mother never won that game.

Then Annie piped up. 'I know a game we can play. Let's see who can stay longest upside down, standing on their hands. I'll go first.'

My mother glanced over at my father, giving him a look and shaking her head. Annie never wore any knickers, and if she was going to be upside down . . . well, it didn't bear thinking about. So she took Annie through to the kitchen and said, 'Annie, you cannae do this, you have no knickers on.'

'Oh, that's ok,' she said, 'I have a safety pin.'

'What good is that going to do?' asked my mother.

'Well,' said Annie, 'I will pin my skirt between my legs, and no one will see anything.' My mother was uncertain, but they went back into the living room again.

'I have to throw myself against the door for support,' Annie said, and she did. She stayed up for a few minutes and then tragedy struck. The safety pin holding the skirt burst open and she didn't notice at first. Ivor ran up to her and tried to cover her with his jacket, but she fell on top of him and dislocated his shoulder. We didn't know he had been hurt, though, and the laughter rang out from all of us.

My father and Ace carried Ivor up to the doctor, who was named Hood and lived not far from us. When Ivor came back, he was all tightly bandaged up. Annie thought we were going to continue the game where we had left off. 'No,' said my mother, 'we have had enough for one night. I will make another cup of tea then we will had awa to bed.'

★

This is a story both my mother and father told. It is a very old, old story indeed.

The Auld Miller

Once upon a time there was a miller and his daughter and they lived on the banks of the Ayr. They had a mill and they took corn in and made it into meal. One day, the miller was walking along the banks of the River Ayr. Just about a field's breadth from his house was the house the laird used to live in. Well, on this day, the laird came walking down the river and he met the old miller. 'Ah, miller,' he said, 'I see you are taking your walk.'

'Oh yes,' said the miller, 'I am takin my walk.'

'And where is your daughter today?'

'Oh, she is workin in the mill.'

The laird said, 'Is she not thinking about getting married yet?'

'Oh no, not yet,' said the miller. 'She is all I've got, and there is nobody else to look after the mill for me!'

'She is a very bonnie girl. I wouldn't mind marrying her myself,' said the laird.

'Oh, I don't know her mind,' said the miller. But he knew she was carrying on with a shepherd boy who stayed in a house on the side of the hill.

So time wore on now, and he met the laird again, and the laird said to him, 'I have been thinking it over, and I will take your daughter's hand in marriage.'

'No, no,' said the miller, 'because she is goin out with the shepherd laddie.'

'Well,' said the laird, 'if you can't give me your daughter, I am afraid you will have to leave your house.'

'Oh,' the miller said, 'is that so?'

'I'll tell you what I'll do,' the laird said. 'I will give you three guesses, and if you can't answer them, you must get out of the house and I will have your daughter.'

'What are the three guesses?' asked the miller.

'Well,' said the laird, 'you must tell me the weight of the moon. The next thing you have to tell me is how many stars there are in the heavens. Thirdly, you must tell me what I am thinking about at that minute.'

'Oh my, my,' said the miller. 'That's three terrible hard ones you have given me.'

'Well,' said the laird, 'If you can't answer them, I get your mill and your daughter as well.'

So the old miller went away home, thinking about these three guesses.

All his work fell behind. The corn was lying there and he could hardly keep his mind on anything else. His daughter asked him three or four times what was wrong. 'Oh, I cannae tell you – you couldn't help me anyway,' he said.

She met the young shepherd that night, and she told him about it, saying she was worried about her father. 'Well,' he said, 'I'll come doon the night and I will have a word wi him. Maybe he will tell me.'

So the daughter went back home and waited for the young shepherd to arrive. When he came in, he looked all round the mill, and saw all the corn lying about. 'What's wrong wi you, miller? Look at all this corn lying aboot; it's no like you.'

'I don't know what's wrong wi me,' said the miller. 'I met the laird, up the river and he gied me three things tae dae, and there's nae way oot o it.'

'What things?'

'Well, the laird wants Annie to be his wife.'

'Oh!' said the shepherd, 'He cannae dae that.'

'He has given me three guesses,' said the miller, 'and I can't answer them. If I don't answer them, he is puttin me out o the mill, and taking Annie for his wife.'

'Let me hear them,' said the shepherd.

'There is nae use me tellin you, for you would never guess them.'

'Let me hear them anyway,' said the shepherd. So the miller explained the questions – the weight of the moon, the number of stars in the heavens, what the laird was thinking at that moment.

'Never mind him at aa, just get on wi your work,' said the laddie. 'When are you meetin him next?'

'On Sunday night,' said the miller, 'when it is getting gloamin dark.'

'Well, come on and I will help you get the corn done.' The laddie helped him grind the corn and they made the meal.

Time wore on till it came to Sunday. The shepherd came down to the miller's house, an hour before the miller had to meet the laird. 'Miller,' said the laddie, 'give me a suit o your auld claes, and I will gang as you.'

The miller said, 'What dae ye mean?'

'Well, I will go in your place, if you give me your auld claes.'

So he put the miller's claes on and marched up the riverside, just as the miller would.

'Well,' said the laird, 'you didn't forget, miller.'

'No, I never forgot, but I didn't think much about them. What were the three guesses again?'

'Well,' said the laird, 'you must tell me the weight of the moon.'

'Oh, that's easy. The moon weighs one ton weight. There are four quarters in the moon, and there are four quarters in a ton.'

'Well done,' said the laird. 'Now, how many stars are there in the heavens?'

'Oh, that's easy – there are 24 million, five hundred and fifty thousand, and if you don't believe me, count them yourself.'

'My goodness,' said the laird, 'you caught me there, but you won't know the next one.'

'What is it then?'

'You must tell me what I am thinking at this very moment.'

'I know that one as well. You think you are speakin tae the auld miller, but you are speakin to the shepherd.'

So the miller kept his mill, and the lad and lass got married.

★

The next Saturday, a fair came to the town and it had a lot of side stalls – the bearded lady, the smallest man and many more. There was also a boxing ring, where you could get money if you beat the boxer. My father bumped into a poor creature called Willie Two. He was speaking to another wee man we called Chinny Chin Chin. The poor man had no chin at all, but he was a wee man who was always laughing and game for anything.

My father said to him, 'How do you and Willie Two no go into the ring and have a fight? The winner gets the pot.' They thought about this for a while, and agreed to have a go, so they went into the ring and the owner put the gloves on them. The news travelled like wildfire and crowds came to watch. They were the funniest sight anybody in Blair had seen for a long time and great entertainment. They were in the ring for about half an hour, and there was one punch thrown from Chinny Chin Chin. He won.

'Where's my pot?' he said.

'Here you are,' said the man in charge, and handed him a saucepan. He eventually saw the funny side of it, and had a good laugh. My father put the hat round everybody, and he got ten shillings.

'No bad', he said, 'for half an oor's work, eh Chin?'

'Great Alex, thank you,' Chin said, and guess what he did? He gave Willy Two half the money, so they got five shillings each and went away as happy as Larry. Neither of them drank, so the chip shop got two good customers that night.

The next day my mother and father took me up to one of the show women to have my ears pierced. Her name was Mrs Taylor and her son Danny, who was about twenty, was awful fond of me. He gave me free rides on the roundabouts, then he carried me home so I could have a lie down, just because my ears had been pierced.

★

My mother had difficulties having her baby. They had opened up a new maternity ward in Meikleour House because the hospital couldn't cope now that there were Polish soldiers who had come to Blair. So my mother went to Meikleour House to have her baby but it was stillborn. My father didn't have a car at the time, so he went out with his pushbike and took the baby home on the back of the bicycle in a wee white coffin. I will never forget that day. He brought the coffin home in the afternoon, but we had to wait until it was dark to bury it. My father, John, Andy, Cathie and myself went to Rattray graveyard and buried my wee sister up against the wall with no marker. She wasn't allowed to be buried in the graveyard itself.

A few days later, my mother came home from the hospital, very sad, as we all were. Ivor and Annie were saving up to go back to Wales where they had come from. On this day they had gone to the berries with Ace, Mickey and Marlene. They picked all day and got two buckets of berries – they should have had more but they weren't good pickers. Ivor came down to the end of the drill carrying the two buckets, and Annie shouted to him to help her with the piece bags. So he left the buckets down at the end of the drill and went to help her, but when he came back there were no berries to be seen. Somebody had stolen them. That made them decide they were going to go home to Wales, even if they hadn't enough money, but my father persuaded them to stay until the end of the berries and to keep a closer watch on their buckets. So that's what they did, and they stayed.

The Sunday of that week my mother made a clootie dumpling. Annie watched her carefully, remembering the ingredients, as she said she was going to make one for Ivor. The next day she went to the shop and bought everything she needed, but she hadn't a muslin cloth to put it in. So she cut off the foot of one of her silk stockings, filled the stocking half-full, tied each end and put it in the pot. I was outside watching her. She was so excited because there was a good smell coming from it. 'Smell that now, Sheila, is that the same smell as Belle's one?'

'Oh aye,' I said, 'just the same.' She took it out of the pot, and it came out like a long sausage. Just then my mother shouted to me, 'Don't ha that mort's habben, mind.' So when Annie offered me a slice, I told her I had just had my tea. When Ivor came home, he thought it was great and scoffed the lot.

While they were living out in the tent in our garden, Annie and Ivor used our toilet. Well, that night he was back and forward all night and no one got a wink of sleep. Poor Ivor, his whole insides were in the toilet.

★

A few months later, my mother fell pregnant again. When the baby was due she was taken to Meikleour House maternity, where she had a baby girl. The nurse brought the baby to her and my mother cuddled it. Then the nurse took it away to give it a bath, came back and said the baby was dead. It had slipped out of her hands, fallen into the bath and banged its head. So it only lived for half an hour. That was the second baby's funeral we had had in the last two years, but this time we were allowed to bury it during the day and it was buried in the proper graveyard.

My mother was still in the maternity ward when a doctor came to her and said they might have a baby for her if she wanted to adopt one. They kept my mother's milk because they thought they could give the baby to her before she left the hospital, but ten days passed and she had to go home. A week later the doctor came to see us and told us they had a ten-day-old baby for us. My mother and I went to a lady from the Red Cross in Perth and collected my new sister. It was the greatest joy of our lives and I was allowed to name her. I chose the name Rena. She was the centre of our world. Nobody can describe the happiness we felt after having lost two babies before.

★

At the end of the berry season, Ivor and Annie went back to Wales and we never heard from them again, but Ace, Mickey and Marlene stayed with us for a few years. At this time, my father was in the pubs a lot. One day, my mother sent my brother John to go and get him out of the pub. They came out of the pub and were walking down the road when they heard screaming behind them. When they turned round, they saw a horse on the rampage coming down past the Well Meadow. My father jumped in front of the horse, grabbed its reins and stopped it. He was deemed a hero that day and the story appeared in many newspapers. When he got home to my mother, though, she didn't make a hero of him. Her long tongue thrashed into him for staying in the pub too long.

Every day, my father went up the glens and round the farms looking for rabbit skins because he got sixpence each for them, which was a good lot of money then. All he had to go round the farms on was a bicycle. He saved the skins up for a week and sold them to Henry Quinn's rag store. He did this for many weeks until he saved enough money to buy a car, which was the first car my father ever had. In those days, you didn't need a licence to drive a car, so my father taught himself. From then on, he worked and we stayed in the fields until he bought a lorry, which gave him the incentive to gather scrap. A year later, he had enough money to buy a piece of land in Old Rattray. He bought a two-bedroom hut and put it on the land, so we left MacDonald Crescent and went to live in there.

★

Berry time was the highlight of each year, with all the travellers coming to pick berries. A farmer had a big hut at Blacklaw, and every Saturday night the travellers held concerts there. There were some great singers and musicians from the travelling community who came and performed. It was like one big travellers' ceilidh. A lot of them got drunk and there was some fighting, but the troublemakers were soon thrown out. In 1947, when I was twelve, my mother wrote her famous song, 'The Berry Fields o Blair'. It is known throughout the world.

The Berry Fields o Blair

When ber - ry time comes roond each year, Blair's po - pu - la - tion's swel- lin. There's ev - ery kind o pick - er there, And ev - ery kind o dwel- lin. There's tents and huts and car - a-vans. There's both - ies and their biv-vies And shel - ters made wi tat-tie bags And dug - outs made wi div -vies.

When berry time comes roond each year,
Blair's population's swellin,
There's every kind o picker there
And every kind o dwellin.
There's tents and huts and caravans,
There's bothies and their bivvies
And shelters made wi tattie-bags
And dug-outs made wi divvies.

There's corner-boys fae Glesgae,
Kettle-boilers fae Lochee,
There's miners fae the pits o Fife,
Mill-workers fae Dundee
And fisherfolk fae Peterheid
And tramps fae everywhere
Aa lookin fir a livin aff
The berry fields o Blair.

There's travellers fae the Western Isles,
Fae Arran, Mull and Skye;

Fae Harris, Lewis and Kyles o Bute,
They come their luck to try.
Fae Inverness and Aberdeen,
Fae Stornoway and Wick
Aa flock to Blair at the berry time,
The straws and rasps to pick.

There's some wha earn a pound or twa,
Some cannae earn their keep,
There's some wid pick fae morn till nicht,
And some wid raither sleep.
There's some wha has tae pick or stairve,
And some wha dinnae care
There's comedy and tragedy
Played on the fields o Blair.

There's families pickin for one purse,
And some wha pick alane,
There's men wha share and share alike
Wi wives wha's no their ane.
There's gladness and there's sadness tae,
There's happy herts and sare,
For there's some wha bless and some wha curse
The berry fields o Blair.

Before I put my pen awa,
It's this I would like to say:
You'll travel far afore you'll meet
A kinder lot than they;
For I've mixed wi them in field and pub
And while I've breath to spare,
I'll bless the hand that led me tae
The berry fields o Blair.

This was the first song my uncle Donald told my mother to
write for our Hogmanay party. That year, as always, it was
wonderful. My mother's song went down a bomb. There were

strangers in the house, first-footing, and they said to my mother's face, 'How can a tink write a song like that?' My uncle Donald and my father weren't long in showing them to the door with a couple of kicks up the arse and you can guarantee they were never allowed in again. From then on, every year, my mother had to write a new song. One year, she wrote a song, 'Glen Isla'. It has never been published before.

Glen Isla

Keen blaws the wind roond the nooks o the shielin,
His auld mallin promise are covered wi sna,
Hoo changed fae the times since we went up Glen Isla,
Lookin for rags or a wee taste o blaw.

We went up by Forter, or maybe the Linns,
Lookin for rags or a wee puckle skins,
Naebody kent on what we had to bear,
The hardships and cauld till we got back tae Blair.

But me and my mother we aye trachled through,
And we aye got the price o a wee taste o brew,
And Donald and Jimmy, they aye did their share
And that was the reason we never left Blair.

Times they have changed, but we cannae help that,
And mony's a nicht when we sit doon tae crack,
We think on wir mither wha noo is awa,
But it's grand tae hae memories that we can reca.

*

My uncle Donald and his wife Jeannie never had any children of their own, only me. So Donald asked my mother to go and see the Red Cross woman in Perth for him so that he and Jeannie could apply to adopt a baby. Two months later they were given one. She was a year old the day they got her. They called her

Alison. At this time, I was practically living with my uncle
Donald and I had a good few ballads under my belt. But from
then on, I wasn't obliged to live there anymore, although I
visited him whenever he remembered a new ballad. The only
ballad my mother would never let me sing, all the time she was
alive, was 'Queen Amang the Heather'. But I used to sing it to
my uncle Donald, without her knowing.

*

My mother and father weren't getting on too well. My mother's
tongue was clippin cloots again and my father was fed up of it,
but he hung in there and tried to ignore her. He took up a new
hobby: going to the pictures every night. She disagreed with his
drinking but going to the pictures was fine. There were two
picture houses in Blairgowrie: the Regal and Quinn's. He could
go from one to the other, seeing a different picture every night.
Sometimes, he didn't have the money to go so took a two-
pound clay jam jar to Quinn's picture house and with Henry
Quinn having a rag store, he accepted this as a ticket.

My mother told my father one night that Ace and Mickey
were leaving. They had got a small house in Montrose and
thought it was time they stood on their own feet. My father was
sad to see Ace go because they had been through Dunkirk
together, but a week later, they left for Montrose. We had the
house back to ourselves then.

My father went to the pub one night and came back drunk.
He climbed into bed and took the horrors of drink. My mother
had to go and get the doctor. When the doctor came, he tied
him with straps to the bed, sent for an ambulance and took him
to Lambert Mental Institution. Two days later, my mother went
to visit him and the doctors told her he was shell-shocked from
the war. It wasn't the drink that started it off – it had been
preying on his mind since Dunkirk. My father was in Lambert
for six months and had electric shock treatment to his brain. It
didn't help, so they stopped it and he gradually recovered by
himself. We visited him twice a week. After the six months were

up, he was allowed to come home but was told to take it easy. His doctor applied for a war pension for him and he was awarded a pension from the army. It was not a lot, but it helped. When he came home, he tried to get us to believe that he had only been kidding us on, because he didn't want his children to think of their father in an asylum. But we all knew the truth.

★

My mother had to sell my father's car when he went into Lambert so that she could buy food for us and pay the bills. When he came out of Lambert, my father gave her ten shillings a day for groceries, but there were seven of us, so that didn't go far. She gradually ran up a huge bill at the grocer's and tried to hide it from my father. But he found out one day and kicked my mother out of the house. She went to the show green up the road, to one of the trailers where her pal Bridget lived. Bridget had been sitting drinking. She had a bottle of whisky, and she and my mother drank it all. Now, my mother was usually no drinker, but that night she was paralytic. My father knew she would be up at Bridget's so he went looking for her. He grabbed her by her hair and kicked her from the show green all the way home. In those days, travelling women never told anybody if they got beaten up by their husbands. My mother stayed in bed for two days, not just from the beating, but also because of a severe hangover after the whisky!

My father decided that the hut we lived in was too small, so he bought a bigger hut that was up for sale in the newspaper from a farmer near Dundee. He, my uncles Donald and Andy and my brother John went and dismantled the sectional hut and brought it home. They used the small hut for firewood. It took them three days to put the new hut together. During this time, we had to sleep in a bus stop – two bus stops actually; one was the bedroom and one was the living room. A week later we moved into the big hut and it was wonderful to have so much space. My mother cooked on a Calor gas stove and we had an outside toilet and an outside tap for water.

My mother was at the tap one day, filling the kettle with water, when a traveller man came up to her and he said he had been watching her for a few weeks. He demanded she run away with him. My mother went straight into the house and told my father. By this time, the man had disappeared. He must have been watching for a long time, because he waited until my father was away hawking and approached my mother again, determined not to take no for an answer. My mother was terrified. When my father came home, he went straight to the police and the next day they put the man in their car, took him to the outside of Blairgowrie, let him out and said he was banned. He was never to come back to Blairgowrie ever again, and he never did.

Six months later, my mother got a letter. It wasn't signed, but it was a love letter and she knew fine it was from him because he came from Inverness and so did the letter. She didn't know whether to tell my father or not because men are funny; even if you tell them nothing happened, jealousy within a man can make them think something did happen, and of course, in this case, it didn't. But in the end, she did tell him because she didn't want to keep any secrets from him. He knew it wasn't her fault, so peace reigned again.

My brother Andy started to buy and sell second-hand cars and advertised and sold them. He made a lot of money. Uncle Donald, Uncle Andy and my brother John also went into the car business. My father sold an odd one now and again, but never really joined them. He preferred hawking and gathering scrap.

*

That Hogmanay, to pass the time till twelve o'clock, we all went to the pictures, except Cathie. When we came home, Cathie was in the house with a traveller man called Jimmy Higgins. His parents lived in Blairgowrie, and he was home on leave. To our great surprise, Cathie announced that she was married to Jimmy. They planned with the minister to be married in his manse on Hogmanay night at six o'clock. She knew we would be at the pictures then, and didn't want my father to stop her. She had only known Jimmy for a week, but a happier couple you couldn't find. Next day, his leave was up and he had to go back to Italy. A few months later, he was demobbed from the army, and they set up house at Rattray Cross.

My brother John, who had got married when I was twelve, had his first baby, a wee boy. He called him after himself, John Stewart. My parents became grandparents then. They were overjoyed. The baby was beautiful, with wee chubby cheeks. Cathie had fallen pregnant at the same time as John's wife and the babies were born a couple of days apart. Cathie's wee boy was named Alex, after my father. My mother said to my father, 'You will have to go up and see your namesake, Alex.' So he went up and looked at the baby, and said to Cathie, 'What tree did you get him aff?' Cathie burst out laughing – she knew my father's sense of humour.

★

My mother was going to the shop one day and bumped into Willy Two. He also stayed in Rattray, in an old road wagon. 'Come doon tae the house tonight, Willie,' she said, 'we are going to tell a few stories, and you will enjoy yourself.'

'Thanks Belle, I will be down.'

That night Willie came in and as usual his face wasn't washed, and he looked scruffy. 'My God,' said my father, 'what have you done to yourself?'

'Well,' said Willie, 'I went hame from the shop, and lit my fire to make myself something to eat. I didn't know these silly boys fae the housing scheme had stuffed divots down my chimney. I thought it was because the sticks were wet and waited for the smoke to clear, but it got worse. So I just left it and came oot doon here. I will wait till it clears and clean the chimney oot tomorrow.'

My mother made him a few sandwiches and tea to keep him going. Poor soul. The stories soon got started. We all loved stories – we had been brought up with them.

My father began.

I mind one time my mother went to Skye. She stayed away down by the shore at a time when travellers stayed in caves and used boats to go round the coast. My mother went out hawking, and she walked and walked and walked till it was coming on grey dark at night.

She said to herself, 'I'll turn back because I ken o a near-cut over the moor.' She spoke to two roadmen working at the side of the road. 'Is this the path that is the near-cut over the moors?'

'Aye, there's a near-cut, but sometimes ye cannae see the path in the dark, and ye might wander off it. It wouldn't be a nice place to wander off across that moor.'

'Oh well,' she said, 'I will chance it anyway, it is nearer than going back to the road.'

So she carried on this sort of bridal path, and walked and walked until she came to an old stead. It had no roof, but there was a chimney at each end. Outside the door there was a big, tall rock. Leaning against it was a young man, and his head was turned the other way. 'It's a fine night,' says my mother.

'Yes, it is a fine night, Missus,' he said.

'This is an awful old building,' my mother said. She loved old historical places, especially old castles.

'It is an old building, alright,' he says. 'There used to be a miner stayed in there.'

'I never thought there would be miners about here,' said my mother.

'It wasn't coal or anything like that,' he said. 'It was silver they used to mine for here. It was an old man that ran the mine, about three or four hundred yards over there,' he said, pointing with his finger. 'The mine working was getting heavy for him and he took on a partner, a young man. Now, the old man was married to a young woman, and one day the old man came up for a drink of water tae the hoose and looked through the window, and saw the young man kissing his wife. He turned on his heel, said nothing and went back down the mine, and set an explosive charge wi a wire on it like a fuse. He came oot o the mine and came running up to the hoose, burst in the door: "I have found riches! A new vein, tons o silver! We are rich, we are rich!"

The boy grabbed his cap and ran oot the door, and just as he went into the mine the blast went off.'

'Was he killed?' asked my mother.

'No,' he said, 'he wasn't. He was able to crawl back to the door, and there he died.'

'He must have been sore hurt,' said my mother.

'Aye,' said the young man, 'the whole side of his face was blowing clean off, just like this,' and he turned to my mother. The side of his face was blown away. She had been speaking to the ghost of the young man.

Now it was Willie's turn to tell a story. 'Come on,' said my mother, 'it's your turn now, Willie.'

'Now,' said Willie, 'I am going to tell you two short stories, that's God's honest truth.' We were all waiting with anticipation. Then he began. 'You know,' he said, 'my sister had a litter of pups to a greyhound, and my brother's thing between his legs was made of gold. When he got hungry he screwed it off and pawned it – oh, he never starved, my brother. Now that's the end of my story.' Well, you can imagine our reaction. We were rolling about the floor laughing. 'Now,' said Willie, 'at least youse got a laugh at my true stories, and I can put my hand on the Bible, they are true.' That finished the night. We were spoiled for telling any more stories, or singing. The laughter took over.

*

Shortly after that time, there was a knock on the door one day and my mother answered it. It was a traveller woman and my mother took her in. 'Belle, I hope you are not annoyed with me for coming here.'

'Not at all,' said my mother. 'What can I do for you?'

'Well, I am going to a weddin and I ken you have a lot of hats. Could I borrow one?'

Now my mother was hat-mad. She hadn't bought many for a few years, but she loved the ones she had. In her younger days, if you didn't wear a hat you were classed as a loose woman.

'Alright,' my mother said grudgingly. Not that she was greedy, but she knew this woman, and if you lent her anything you never got it back. 'Now Jessie,' said my mother. 'I want this hat back when the wedding is over.'

'Oh dear, aye,' said Jessie, 'the next day after the wedding I will bring it right round to you.'

She took the hat and off she went. Two weeks passed. No hat. A month passed, no hat. Two months later, my mother was walking down to Blair when there in front of her was the woman Jessie, wearing the hat. Well, my mother went over to her and tore the hat off her head. She had it pinned down with two hat-pins, but my mother still ripped it off, hair and all. The woman was screaming holy blue murder, but my mother couldn't have cared less. She finally got her hat back.

*

We all went on holiday together every year to Aberfeldy, which was one of our favourite places. My mother's brother Donald, his wife, her brother Andy and his wife, and all my cousins came too. Just before Aberfeldy, there was a farm on the hill. The farmer let us camp there every year, and we could stay as long as we liked. This year we had a small 'whoopee' caravan – about twelve feet long – for my dad, Mum, Rena and me.

We arrived on a Monday afternoon. We all had caravans and it was the first time we had never had to put up tents. We still had a fire, which was our focal point, and where everyone gathered. It was a lovely day, just after the berry-picking season. My mother and my auntie Jeannie took their buckets to go for water and coming back as they neared the incline to get to the caravans, Jeannie slipped and slid on her arse for about five yards right into a cow pat, then kept sliding and hit another one. She was covered from head to foot in cow shit. Well, she got up and hurried to where the fire was, shouting, 'Donald, look at me! What am I going to dae?'

All he could do was burst out laughing at her, everyone at the same time. The stench coming from her was unbearable. She got angry and started to argue with my uncle Donald, asking him to take her home. My mother said to her, 'Come on wi me and we will go doon tae the burn and get a wash and a change.'

But no, she wanted to go home. She argued for ages, then calmed down, and fell silent for a while.

'Alright,' Donald said, 'I will take you hame.'

'No you won't,' she said, 'I'm staying.'

That really upset Donald. 'Alright, if that's how you want it.' He went into the caravan, took a mattress off the bed and threw it at her.

'You stay, I am going hame without you.' Real angry he was. My mother went over to him and talked for ages and calmed him down. So he stayed. Round the fire that night, Jeannie finally saw the funny side of it, and laughed her head off.

We stayed there for two weeks then returned home. We all called ourselves a wagon train, following each other down the road. My father was driving in front of the others. A few miles down the road on a small hill, a caravan passed us.

'Look, Belle, there is a caravan wi no car.'

'You fool, Alex, that's our caravan!'

It must have come loose from the car, so we followed it down the hill until we saw it disappear over a drop at the side of the road. My father stopped and looked over and it was hanging by a thread, pinned to a tree for support – it hadn't quite gone over the cliff. Donald and Andy appeared with a tow rope and my father scrambled down to the caravan and tied the rope to it. He came back up, tied it to the car and pulled it up. It was some holiday that year, I can tell you – a holiday we never forgot and we had a good laugh about it when we got home.

★

Now I am going to do something that has never been done on paper before by a traveller. I am going to try to write down something that has been lost long ago. Some pipers may know it still, but only played on the pipes. It's my mother's cantarach: syllables made by the mouth. Well, here goes. I hope I can manage it.

Hidery haetin tao hebidum buderum tachum ti
Hidery haetin tao hi ba dachum hider tae o hachum
Hidery haetin tae o hebadum buderm tachin ti
Hidery haetin hao hi bi diddy hi chumm biddera.

Halady hacharum teacherum tallady hint ady
Hecherum techerum hallady hin ta dae
Hecherum techerum tallady dae hint ady
Habidy hi a hach a ra ra.

Well, that was very, very difficult to put down on paper. It sounds like a different language. No doubt many people who read this book have either heard my mother, or me, performing it at some point.

★

In later years, we didn't go back to Aberfeldy as a wagon train. Instead, we went up to Banff to visit our friends Frank and Ruby Kelbie. One year, my father bought a Hillman car in Old Deer. I was fifteen at the time and had to drive it home for him, with Frank's brother Willie Kelbie in the car with me for company. When we arrived home that day, Willie Kelbie said to me, 'By God, Sheila, you can fair drive. How long have you been driving for?'

'Willie,' I said, 'this is the first time I have been at the wheel of a car in my life.' Well, he turned green and was sick all over the road. I never did that again, believe you me.

My mother made up a song about that time:

Frank and Ruby

> Frank and Ruby bide in Banff
> And Kelbie is their name,
> It's them that we aye bide wi
> When we gang awa fae hame.

For I can go tae Ruby's hoose
Though it be the deed o nicht,
And she strips the bed claes aff her bed
To see that we're aa richt.

And Frank he never gang tae work
As lang as we are there
And nae doot there's mony a time he's cursed
His freens that come fae Blair.

We went to Peterhead one day
It was an awfa rain.
We bought a Hillman in Auld Dear
And Sheila drove it hame.

We had a dram the nicht afore
And Frank's een they were ticht
For he tried tae sort an organ
But he could nae sort it richt.

Noo, we've had freens afore, ye ken,
But they werena just the same,
We can gang tae you at ony time
And mak wirsels at hame,

But we'll be back gin Hogmanay
As sure as I am here,
So you better hae your cupboard full
O guid strong drink and beer.

Frank and Ruby came down often because we had the wee
trailer and they stayed in that. It was Ruby who gave my mother
and I the song 'Banks of Red Roses'. In it, a boy kills his
girlfriend because she is becoming too serious about him. Ruby
couldn't remember all of the song, but these are the verses she
taught us.

Banks of Red Roses

Noo, when I was a young thing, and easy led astray,
Afore that I would work I would rather sport and play,
And afore that I would work I would rather sport and play
Wi' my Johnny on the banks amang red roses.

On the banks of red roses, my love and I sat doon,
And he took oot his charm-box to play his love a tune,
In the middle o the tune his love broke doon and cried,
'Oh, my Johnny, lovely Johnny, dinna leave me.'

He took oot his pocket knife, and it been long and sharp,
And he pierced it through and through his bonnie lassie's heart,
And he pierced it through and through his bonnie lassie's heart,
And he left her lying there among red roses.

My mother had an argument one day with a man who stayed next door to us. He said my father was disturbing the peace, because he was sawing up logs to sell for money to feed us. Well, my mother went mad at him and chased him from our door with a brush. He ran like the wind, terrified. Later on that day, his wife came to my mother and apologised for him, saying he had a bad temper. 'I'll give him a bad temper,' said my mother.

'Well, you know he gets annoyed with you kind o lads,' she said.

'What do you mean?' my mother said.

'You kind o lads – I mean tinks.' Well, my mother chased her for her life and she flew back into her house. And we didn't see them for about a week after that.

*

Between his berry fields, selling scrap and pearl-fishing the Tay and the Dochart, my father saved enough money to build a bungalow in place of the hut we were living in. He got the plans drawn up and a builder came from Montrose to build it. There were three bedrooms, a living room, a kitchen and a bathroom. While it was being built, Rena, my parents and I lived in our trailer and we eventually moved into the bungalow in about 1952. My father's mother had died from a brain haemorrhage a few years earlier, so my father's father came to stay with us in the bungalow. He was an old man by this time – eighty-three. He wasn't well, but with my mother's nursing he got a lot better. He was no bother to look after at all – he had a great sense of humour and was always cheery.

This is a pipe tune he had written when he was much younger, back in 1908.

Iain Mhor

*

I remember a trip to Ireland with my parents and my grandfather. The four of us had decided to go to Carrigans, where my parents' best friends, Mosie Ray and his sister Maggie lived. We took over a caravan to live in, because a tent wouldn't have been appropriate for my grandfather – he was getting too old by this time.

We arrived in Carrigans in the afternoon and found a place to put our trailer. Then we all went into the town and my father and my grandfather headed straight to Mosie's house, with my mother and I following them. My mother asked, 'How do you know this is the house? He may have moved by this time.'

'Na,' said my father, 'this is it alright.' So he knocked on the door, and an old man of about sixty appeared.

'Oh my God,' he said, 'Alex and Jock! Come away in.' So we all went into the house, and I may say we have never been made to feel so welcome in our lives. The kettle was put on straight away by his wife and then she went next door for some scones and biscuits.

Mosie told my mother all that my father had got up to during the time they had been separated. There was nothing too bad, but he did tell the story of Katie, a girl in Carrigans my father was taking out, who had 'awful sore eyes'. She had no eyelashes, and every day a scab would gather on her eyes. Mosie explained, 'She wasn't bad looking, but o her eyes.'

Seemingly, everyone made a fool of my father for going out with her at all, so when he broke up with her, he said they were moving on. She looked at him and said, 'Tell me, Alex, why did you go out with me in the first place?'

My father didn't want to hurt her, because she was a nice girl. So he said, 'It's your eyes, ducky. It's your eyes.'

She smiled, and said, 'Thank you, Alex.' She knew he was trying to be kind.

'Where's your sister Maggie now?' my grandfather asked.

'Oh, her, she is still in Carrigans. She got married you know, to a farmer. He has money and she has risen above her station. That woman is a pain. We don't speak much these days, just a nod in the passing. I think you should go up to the farm and see her. She will be fine with you, and she will be glad to see you all, sure.'

My mother looked at my father and winked. She turned to old Mosie and said, 'Mosie, we were wondering if it would be alright to have a ceilidh in your house tomorrow night.'

His eyes beamed bright. 'You mean like the old days?'

'Yes,' my mother said. 'Like the old days.'

'Oh, my blessings be on you for makin an old man happy! Maybe it's the last time we will ever see each other again. By the Holy Mary, thank you.'

He explained where Maggie's farm was and so we headed there the next day. It was in among some trees on a hill and there was an old track road up to it for about half a mile or so. Hens and ducks were running all over the yard in front of the house. Before we went in, my father said to my mother, 'What was all the winking about in auld Mosie's house?'

'Well,' said my mother, 'I had an idea that if we held a ceilidh in his house, and asked Maggie to come, maybe we could get them on speaking terms again.'

'And here's me thinking you were going to crown me for going with that other lassie,' said my father.

'Dinnae flatter yourself, wee man. That was in the past.' My father hated to be called 'wee man', so she had managed to get her own back on him.

The mess from the hens was terrible and we had to watch where we were walking to get to the door. My mother knocked, and we waited a few minutes, then heard a voice saying, 'Come in, whoever's there, because I can't come out, sure.'

So in we walked, and she was sitting on a chair about five feet away from the fire, with her hands full of flour, making dough. She threw the dough onto the griddle from where she was sitting and it landed there perfectly.

'Oh dear, dear, am I seeing right? Is that you, Jock and Alex? Oh my, I thank the blessed Virgin this day,' Maggie said. 'Come in and sit down. You must have smelled my scones all the way from Scotland. Ha ha ha!' She laughed in the funniest way, as if she was gasping.

We all sat down except my grandfather. He asked her if he could have a drink of water. So she scurried away – that was the only way you could describe her walk – and fetched him a drink of water in a cup. 'Thanks,' he said to her. She talked and talked, ten to the dozen and you could tell she was pleased to see us. My grandfather drank some of the water and threw the rest along the carpet.

'What are you doin min,' asked my father, 'throwin the water all over the woman's floor?'

'Oh Maggie, I am so sorry,' my grandfather said. 'I thought I was at the camp, and you ken we throw wir tea and water leavings in the grass.'

'That's alright Jock,' she said, 'my carpet is needing a good wash anyway, wi the hens' shit in the morning and all that rubbish we trail in with our feet.'

My mother spoke while Maggie was taking the clort (that's the local word they used for griddle scones) out of the pan. 'We are having a ceilidh the night Maggie, would you like to come?'

'Oh yes, of course I would, me and my man. He went out an hour ago to feed the hens, and hasn't come back yet.'

'We never seen him out there,' said my father.

'No you wouldn't, because he will be asleep in one of the sheds as usual, lazy bugger that he is. Oh, but he is a fine man. I get everything my own way. We have two acres here, you know. It's a big farm we got. There is nothing in the field yet. He was going to plant it, five years ago, but he has never got round to it yet. Maybe someday,' she said.

Just like that, the man came in, and was pleased to see us. He had wondered who the car belonged to. 'My name is Jerry,' he said. He went round the room shaking everyone's hand in a courteous manner. 'Have our visitors had tea yet, Maggie?'

'No,' she said. 'I was waiting till the clorts were ready. The last one is in the pan now. You get the cups out, Jerry.'

He looked at her with shock on his face. 'But we only have two cups, as you know.'

'Well, give them to the woman and the girl. The men can use jam jars.'

The clort was the best I have ever tasted, but by the look on my father's and my grandfather's faces, they were less happy. It wasn't that they had never drunk out of jam jars before. Rather, it was their heat that made them very difficult to hold and there was no table to put them on. My family was brought up, for hygiene reasons, not to put cups on the floor because they had to go in our clean-dish basin. Although Maggie said, 'Put them on the floor sure, if it is too hot to hold,' they didn't, so they burned their hands. My mother and I couldn't help but laugh at them.

'Now,' said Maggie, 'where is this ceilidh you are having tonight?'

My father swallowed hard and said, 'It's in Mosie's house.'

'What,' she said, 'in that old fungus man's house? You won't get me there.'

'Now listen,' said my mother, 'We were at him yesterday and we asked him to have it in his house and he said yes. This may be the last time you will see us again, and we want to make it like old times. Please Maggie, say you'll come. Jock's getting no younger and he wants the two of you there, please.' Maggie thought for a while. You could actually hear the motors in her brain working.

'Very well,' she said, 'I'll come, but I'm no speaking to that dirty scoundrel Mosie.'

'You don't have to, if you don't want to,' said my mother. 'It is starting about seven, because Jock can't sit up too late.'

'We will be there, won't we Jerry?' she said to her husband. He nodded.

We got to Mosie's about quarter to seven as we wanted to be there before Maggie came in. When we arrived, there were already ten people in the house who had come for the ceilidh. It was up to my father to break the news to Mosie and his wife that Maggie was coming as well. The expression on Mosie's face was a picture. Then he looked at my father, sternly. 'If she starts any of her nonsense, I will flatten her, and send for the guards to arrest her.'

'It won't come to that,' said my mother. 'We are here for a night of music and song.' That seemed to calm him down.

There was a knock at the door. I can tell you, our hearts were in our mouths, waiting to see what would happen. Mosie's wife answered the door and in came Maggie, with a face on her as if she had been sucking lemons for a week. Jerry toddled in behind her. They sat down without speaking to anyone and never glanced over once to where Mosie was seated. My mother jumped in quickly. 'I think I will sing you an Irish song,' she said. They had never heard my mother sing before, and a hush spread all over the room. She began.

Black Waterside

As I walked out one evening, so early as I strayed,
'Twas in the merry month of June and the birds sang in each
    shade,
And the sun it shone melodiously, and decked all in her pride,
With the primroses and daisies, down by Black Waterside.

I had not walked more than a mile, when there a pair I spied,
Two lovers walked as they did talk down by Black Waterside,
He entwined his arms around her waist, and this to her he said,
'It's in America I'll prove true, to my lovely Irish maid.'

'When you go to America and those Yanky maids you see,
If they be fair and handsome there, you'll forget your love for me,
You'll forget all your vows and your promises, just unto me
    you've made,
So stay at home, and do not roam, from your lovely Irish maid.'

'When I go to America, and those Yanky maids I'll see,
If they be fair and handsome there, they'll remind me just on
    thee,
For there's not a flower grows in yon bower, in yon mountain
    valley or shade,
But will me remind of you behind, my lovely Irish maid.'

'But many the lad has left his home, bound for a foreign shore,
They have left their wives and their own sweethearts, their
    faces to see no more.
While sailing o'er the wide Atlantic, in the sea their body was laid,
So stay at home, and do not roam, from your lovely Irish maid.'

'Now to reflect that you are alone, I will never cross the tide,
And if it be with your own consent, I'll make you my bride,
And we will spend our days in happiness down by Black
Waterside.'

Well, there wasn't a dry eye in the house, and when we looked
over Mosie was holding Maggie's hand. 'Come here you old
bugger,' she said and threw her arms around his neck and kissed
him on the cheek.

His wife gave a sigh of relief. 'I have waited a long time for
this. Now we can be a family again, praise be.'

I was happy and felt like singing a wee cheery ditty.

> If you have the toothache,
> And greetin wi the pain,
> Dinnae buy bags o sweeties,
> For that's a silly game.
> Fill your mouth wi water,
> And mix wi caster oil,
> And put your arse upon the fire,
> Till it begins to boil.

Well, they all started laughing, and I had to teach everyone in the
room the words.

Next day we had to leave Ireland, but we were proud of what we had achieved. I bet Mosie and Maggie didn't forget it in a hurry. We never saw them again, but we heard a few years later that Mosie, that great old man, had died.

★

I will never forget my grandfather's last Christmas on earth. It was Christmas Eve, 1953, and it was snowing outside. Huge flakes, as big as half crowns, were falling very gently to the ground. We had our curtains wide open, and the carol singers appeared from nowhere, and stood outside our window. The minister was with them. My father went out with a bottle of sherry and gave them all a glass. He also gave them money for the church, although they would not allow travellers inside a church in those days.

I saw tears come to my grandfather's eyes that night. 'This is the best Christmas I have had in a long time.' We opened the window and my grandfather leaned out and shook the minister's hand.

It was the most wonderful present we got that year, because we knew we wouldn't have him for long. He even cracked a few jokes, and cantarached the 74th's 'Farewell to Edinburgh' while heating himself at the fire. We could see he was getting tired, so my father took him to bed and tucked him in. 'Thanks Alex,' he said, 'that was a bra night.'

My father left him and wandered outside to be on his own. It was a very emotional night for him too.

1954–1980

In March 1954, Hamish Henderson found out that my grandfather, the great Jock Stewart, was living with us, so he asked if he could come to our house and record him speaking. He knew he couldn't play the pipes any more, but he wanted to ask him some questions about his piping. Hamish asked him about various pipers by name and he said he liked them all – they were all good friends. Hamish asked him about a particular piper, whose name I can't remember. 'What like o piper was he, Jock?'

'Well,' my grandfather said, 'if he played a good march, he played a bad reel, and the other way roond.'

My grandfather also told Hamish a story about a whitterick – a weasel – and a crow.

The Whitterick and the Crow

I went up to Hannah's Farm. I was going to work at the tatties. There was a tattie pit aside where I was workin. An auld crow was dabbin away at this tattie and as I watched it, I saw a whitterick comin oot. It was watchin this auld crow and all of a sudden it made a dart right on the crow's back. Now, didn't the crow start flyin! It went up and up and up and the whitterick's got its teeth intae the crow's neck and it was killin it. The crow died up there and do you know what the whitterick did? It got the two wings o the deid crow and it glided down to the ground again, the whitterick sittin on the back o the dead crow. That was the queerest thing I had ever seen.

Readers can decide for themselves whether they think this story is true or not, but my grandfather swore it was. Hamish Henderson taped this story, but my grandfather's speech wasn't too good and it was very difficult to make out what he was saying. Later that year, my grandfather died. The day before his death, he was in his bed and he asked my father to get the chanter. He made my father blow the chanter while he put his fingers on the holes and tried to play a tune, which he couldn't manage. But it pleased him no end that he had the chanter in his hand.

My mother was destroyed by the death – that was another generation gone. My grandfather's funeral was very large. He was buried in Alyth and he was piped from the bottom of the avenue in Alyth, right to the graveside. It was a very sad day for us all.

Loch Duich

As I was walking with my lover,
Down a glen that was so fair,
There I heard a piper playing,
And his music filled the air.

As I listened to the music
And it sounded loud and clear,
I sat doon among the heather,
Wi the lass that I loved dear.

The tune he played it was 'Loch Duich',
That's a grand auld Scottish air,
There I wooed and won my lassie,
Amang the heather bloomin fair.

All my friends are wildly scattered,
Some I'll never see again,
Others they have left their homeland,
For to sail across the main.

But I hope we'll be together,
As we were so long ago,
When I heard that piper playin,
In the valley of Glen Coe.

★

In March 1954, Hamish Henderson invited us to do a concert in Edinburgh. There was my mother, my father, Cathie and myself, Jeannie Robertson, Jimmy MacBeath and the Auld Galoot, Davie Stewart. The concert was held in an old church and we had to perform from the pulpit one at a time. At the end of the concert we all went back to Hamish's flat. There was also a folk group there and the boys had no money for petrol to get back home to Glasgow so they came back to Hamish's flat to be paid, as we all did. Hamish was a wee bit worse for wear from drink and he said he had no cheques left to pay us. One of the men in the folk group was a solicitor and he said to Hamish, 'You don't need cheques.' He went through to the toilet and he brought back one piece of toilet paper for every artist. He made Hamish sit at his desk and write a cheque out on each piece of toilet paper.

'Now,' he said, much to Hamish's annoyance, 'the bank will take that.' And sure enough, the bank took it as a cheque. It wasn't a lot in those days: we got five pounds each for our concert, twenty pounds in all, and my father got two pounds for his petrol. That was the first public concert we ever did as the Stewarts of Blair.

Hamish Henderson opened the door for us to come out of our seclusion and be accepted by society as having something to offer them, but only in the folk scene. My mother and father often said they thanked Hamish for doing this because at least some folk in the world accepted us for what we were.

We picked the berries that year on the second week in July and many collectors from America came to try to record us. Hamish pitched his tent at my brother's field, the Cleaves. His future wife, Kätzel, and her sister also came berry-picking that year and also pitched their tent at the Cleaves. It was here that she and Hamish met and fell in love.

One day, my mother, my uncle Donald and I went out to the Cleaves to watch the folk picking. Uncle Donald was weighing the berries and I was paying out the money. My mother was away down at the camps, blethering to some of the berry-pickers. It was quite a cold day and this wee boy came up the drill with a small bucket full of berries. He gave them to Uncle Donald to weigh. He had a long drip at his nose, and as he stood there waiting, he took the cuff of his jumper and wiped it across his nose to get rid of the drip. I saw his cuff was stiff. I turned round and looked at Hamish. He also had a drip at his nose and he looked me straight in the eye, lifted up his arm, wiped his nose on his cuff, same as the wee boy, and said to me, 'Sheila, when in Rome . . .'

That year, because we had electricity, many berry-pickers came to our house at night so Hamish could record them. Among them were the Brazils. Auld Weenie Brazil was a great clogger and carried his board around with him. Hamish recorded the noise he made with his feet and listening to it, you would never notice there were no instruments playing. His feet made all the music. Angelina, his daughter, was a great singer and recorded many songs for Hamish. There were always people who came to our house to be recorded and they are too numerous to mention. We always ended the night with my father playing the pipes. That year was the best year we had ever had at the berries. Hamish sometimes brought a bottle of whisky to start the night, put it down on the table and said to my mother, 'There's a dram for ye, Belle.' None of us really drank, so Hamish would end up scoffing the bottle himself. Periodically, he would slide under the table for at least ten minutes and come up again a wee bit more sober, then have another swig out of the bottle. One night when everybody went home, Hamish slept under the table. He had a terribly sore back in the morning! These gatherings went on the six weeks of the berry-picking. The material Hamish got, he said 'was like holding a bucket under Niagara Falls'.

★

Jim Reid, who was and still is one of the best friends of our family, wrote this tune for us.

The Stewarts of Blair

★

We were once asked to go to a club in Newcastle, I think it was in 1954, before I was married, and we were booked in at a hotel for the night, but we arrived too late and had to go straight to the club to perform. When the night was over, we asked the directions to the hotel. Nowadays, the organisers would have taken us there, but they didn't then. We got lost. It was very late and the street was practically empty so, when he saw a man on the other side of the road, my father jumped out of the car.

'Hi, min!' he shouted to the man. The man turned and saw this big man dressed in all his Highland regalia and took off as fast as he could! My sister Cathie went out the next time and asked a couple where the hotel was. 'You are here,' they said, pointing to the hotel.

'Thank God,' said my mother, because we were all tired by this time, especially my father who had driven all the way down from Blair.

My mother and father's room was on the first floor. Cathie and I had to go up to the top landing to a room with 'fire escape' written on the door. It was a fine room with two beds in it, but there was a wee smell of burning. On the dressing table was the biggest Bible we had ever seen. We went down to my mother and father's room to see if they had a big Bible in theirs too, but they didn't. My father chased us up to our own room. 'Go up you thickened lassies, and gie us peace.'

So up the stairs we went, opened the door slowly and went in. We got into our beds and Cathie put the light out. No sooner was it off when she put it back on again. 'I am not comfortable in this room,' she said. 'Come on in beside me, I'm frightened.'

So I crawled in beside her and put the light out, and we heard something at the wall beside our bed. Then the scraping started at the window – scrape, scrape, scrape. Well, you can imagine how terrified we felt! We tried to go to sleep, but we couldn't.

We came downstairs at eight o'clock after having drifted off for an hour because daylight had finally come in and the scraping had stopped. We met my mother and father in the dining room having their breakfast. We couldn't speak when we first came in, but the waitress overheard our explanation to my parents. She came and looked at us. 'Were you two in the room at the top?'

'Yes,' we said.

'Oh my goodness, no one has been in there since the accident.'

'What accident?' my mother asked.

'There was a young woman in that room when it caught on fire, and she couldn't get out. She was burned to death, and was found the next day lying at the window with blood on her nails. The window was all scraped – she was trying to get out.'

'That', said my father, 'was why the Bible was in the room.'

'That's the first time there has been anyone in that room since it happened, and they have painted it a few times, but they can't get the smell of burning to go away,' the girl explained.

Well, you can believe me or not. We never saw anything, but, by God, we heard it. My father still thought we were kidding on, but my mother finally persuaded him that we weren't. We went many times to Newcastle after that night, but from then on we stayed with the folk who ran the club.

★

That year, Old Douglas Kennedy and his wife turned up and stayed with us for a few weeks. They had a motor home and they parked it in our yard. Their son Peter arrived the next day with his wife and we took them all pearl-fishing on the Tay. They got some seed pearls and a few brown ones and were thoroughly delighted. Old Douglas Kennedy was one of the nicest people we had ever met, and so was his wife. The next day, Peter started to record our singing. He got a lot of material from my mother and the rest of us.

After they left a few weeks later, my father decided he wanted to sell his berry field at Essendy. He also wanted to sell the bungalow and asked my brother Andy if he would buy it. When my father built the bungalow, it had cost him £1,800 to build. Andy offered him £3,000 for it. I was curious and asked my father why he wanted to sell off everything and he said that he, my mother and Rena were going off to Canada to live near his brother Andrew. That was a great shock for the family. My father and mother moved out of the bungalow into a small house in Montrose and booked their passage for Canada. My brother Andy moved into the bungalow with his family. My parents had to go to a doctor to have vaccinations before they left and my father took a horrible reaction to one of the injections. The doctor said his blood wasn't right and that he wasn't allowed to go to Canada, so that swept their plans under the carpet.

They came back to Blair and my father bought a row of houses in New Alyth. I was married at that time with four children and we lived in Alyth itself. The row of houses my father had bought was empty except for the one that my parents and Rena lived in, so we moved to New Alyth and took one of the houses. Cathie and Jimmy and their family moved into another one, a Glasgow family moved into another one and my mother's cousin got the last one. My mother and father had many ceilidhs in the house and met all sorts of people who stayed in our back gardens in caravans and tents. With two other folk singers, my father discussed the idea of starting a festival in Blairgowrie. He tried to persuade them it was a great idea and that it was what Blairgowrie needed. They said they would think about it.

*

To the traveller's eye, my mother's cousin's husband Peter was too 'womanified'. When he did the cooking, he put a woman's apron on. To my mother that was a disgrace. She had an argument with him one day about him being too effeminate and went charging down to her own house, came back with a woman's apron and a pair of her big bloomers with elastic in the legs. She went up to their door, opened it and threw them in his face. 'Now Peter,' she said, 'take the hint!'

His wife, my mother's cousin Sissy was a seamstress and she sat at her sewing machine all day filling in orders she got from the public. She was a bit of a hypochondriac and it was she who had moulded Peter into being feminine because he was made to do all the work in the house. She was fuming when she heard what my mother had done. She ran out of her house and came down to my mother's to argue. My mother was standing outside her back door when Sissy arrived on the scene. She caught Sissy by the hair, threw her down on the ground and rubbed her face in the mud. She grabbed her by the shoulders and tore her up and down a big muddy puddle. Then she brushed off her hands and went back into her house. Next day, Sissy came to her door and asked my mother up for a cup of tea. Our travelling family never held grudges; we were brought up that way. One day you could have a good old rumble, and the next day you were speaking to your enemy.

★

The Glasgow folk that moved in next door to my mother were a really nice family. There was an old woman, her daughter and her husband and their four children. The old woman loved her dram – it was Special Brew she drank. My father had a van then and he was going up to Alyth one day with my mother when the old woman came out of her house. She asked my father to give her a lift up the road. So my father opened the back doors of the van and she jumped in. Her clothes went up above her head and she had no knickers on. My father was mortified, and he said, 'I saw everything there!'

The old woman said, 'You saw Campbeltown Loch.'

From that day until the day she died, she was never known as anything else but Campbeltown Loch. She was a great singer and, when she had had a few drinks, she and my mother would sit out on the grass in the back garden and swap songs.

We stayed there, in New Alyth, for a good few years. One thing that stands out in my mind about New Alyth was that every Hogmanay after twelve o'clock, my father would blow up his pipes, leave his house and walk all the way round New Alyth. Everybody in the houses joined us; it was a parade every Hogmanay and it was the highlight of the year.

Around that time, my father told me one of his stories.

The Three-fitted Pot

Once upon a time there was a traveller man an a traveller woman. They had naethin in the world. But he was a peaceful livin man, he never did any harm, never was in jail, he jist lived tae travel roon the countryside wi his wife an two weans. He could make baskets an tin, play the pipes, sing songs an he was a great man for throwin the stane an playin quoits, a great sportsman. An it was a hard time wi them.

They're travelling away up this back glen an they hadnae as much as wad make tea tae theirsels an the weans were gaspin wi the hunger. He made twa baskets wi green wands – he never peeled them – an he says tae his wife, 'If ye can sell thae twa baskets, we could maybe get something. God knows whether there's a shop.'

'Well,' she says, 'I'll try my best.' They came up this road an there was a bit o a fairm. 'Try', he says, 'if there's a man at aa, an ask him if he's a bit o tobacco. I'm dyin for a smoke!'

The woman goes to the fairm an raps at the door an oot comes this big tall woman. 'What dae ye want?' she says.

'I've twa weans doon there,' says the traveller woman, 'an ma man. We're dyin o starvation.'

'Oh dear,' says the woman. 'That's no sae guid. What's that ye've got there?'

'That's two baskets, mistress,' says the traveller woman.

'That's the very thing I was needin tae gaither ma eggs. Come away in an I'll gie ye something for the weans an yersel.'

She took her intae the kitchen o the fairm an it was spotless and beautiful. She gien her tea an sugar, milk an scones an meal, a puckle o floor an a big lump o ham. 'If ye wait till ma man comes in, I'll gie ye a puckle tatties.'

'Oh,' says the traveller woman, 'that's fine. I'll tell ye wan thing. Ma man's never had a smoke for days an he's dyin for a smoke.'

'Oh,' says the woman, 'I'll gie ye a smoke.' An she went intae a caddy on the mantelpiece an gien the woman a lump o tobacco.

'Aw, thanks very much, ma'am,' says the traveller woman.

'Where are ye gaun tonight?' asks the farmer woman.

'Oh we'll go up the glen an maybe gat a place tae stop,' she says.

'If ye go up there,' says the fairmer woman, 'there's an auld wastins that was wan o the plooman's hooses an it tumbled doon. Ye'll get strae for your bed an ye can bide there as long as ye like.'

'Thanks very much,' says the woman. She went doon the road an telt her man this an they went up an found this wastins, an put up their tent. 'What a beautiful place for the tent,' he says, 'wi clean water an everythin running by there.'

'Now,' says the woman, 'we've nae dishes. If I had ony kind o pot I could boil they tatties.'

'Aye,' he says, 'that's richt.' An he's away roon the auld hoose. The cupboards were still there belonging tae the folk an there was naethin in them till he came to wan an there was a three-fitted pot in it, beautiful and clean, jist like a shillin inside.

'That's the very thing,' she says, an she took it tae the burn and scour't it clean wi a sod. Then she boiled the tatties in it. 'Thank God for that pot,' she says, 'a thing I was needin aa ma days.' She washed it clean an pit it upside doon on top o their barra an they went tae their beds.

They were lyin in their bed maybe a couple o oors, when they heard a rumble outside. She says 'Hey, man, hey!'

'Whit is it?' he says.

'There's something oot there tryin tae steal ma pot.'

'Awa,' he says, 'Ye're mad! Wha wad come trailin up the glen tae steal your pot?'

They soon fell soun asleep again. The pot got off the barra, awa up the road tae the big hoose! Next day, there was going to be a big shoot an the chef was makin a dinner for aa these gillies an things, wi partridges, pheasants and hens an this great roast. The pot goes intae the kitchen where the chef was working. 'I wonder,' he says, 'where I can put this roasted leg o mutton?' He looks an he sees the pot an he says, 'The very thing!'

He puts the leg o mutton intae it an awa tae his bed. Doon the pot came tae the road an tae where the barra was. Next day when she got up, the woman looked for her pot.

'Aw,' she says, 'hey, man! Come here tae ye see whit's in the pot!' This was the roasted leg o mutton. 'Maybe the woman of the fairm took pity on us an cam doon an left this for the weans.'

'Oh,' he says, 'that's what it must hae been.'

That nicht, the woman boiled mair tatties in her pot an they ate them wi the leg o mutton. Then she washed the pot again an put it on top o the barra an they went tae their bed again.

They're just sleepin when the pot goes off on its three legs an makes for the castle. It goes in the back door an up a lobby tae where the auld gentleman o the castle is sittin at a table countin his money. Sovereigns an half sovereigns an gold trinkets! He's looking for a place tae pit them in when he'd counted them an he sees the pot. 'Aw, just a fine thing,' he says, 'tae haud ma money.' An he's in wi the sovereigns intae the pot an he rises tae go away for something else an the pot striggles oot the door an back tae the tent.

When the man and woman got up in the morning an the man went tae the pot tae look at it, he nearly fainted! He gien a roar an hold his hairt. 'Jeannie, come here tae ye see thin! We're quadded, we're quadded!'

'What is it, Jack?' she says.

'The pot's hauf full o lour!'

They ended up arguin aboot where the money had come fae. They waited but naeobdy came, so he took a big cloot an emptied the sovereigns oot, tied them up in the cloth an left them in the bottom o the barra an pit a puckle straw on top o't. 'We'll wait for a day to see if anybody comes an if they speak aboot it I'll show them where it is an tell them I put it in there for safety.'

They waited a day but nobody came. That nicht they went tae bed. 'Hey man,' she says, 'rise an look at the pot.'

'The pot's there!' he says.

'Just rise an take wan look at it!' she tells him.

'Awa,' he says, 'I'm mad wi you an your pot! God hear my prayer, I wish you'd never seen that pot. I hope someone takes that pot awa fae ye tae I get peace!'

The next day when they got up, the pot wasnae tae be seen! It was away!

'There, noo,' she says, 'I telt ye there was somebody knockin aboot this camp. Ma wee pot's away an I wadnae hae lost that wee for any money!'

They never saw the pot again. Next day they went awa doon the glen wi their wee barra an this cloot full o gold sovereigns. Whatever happened tae them I dinna ken, but I never met them since. I could dae wi meeting them tae get a shillin or twa off them!

★

We were at the berry-picking one day up at Marshall's of Alyth. They had the best berries all around the area, and Mr Marshall was a great boss to work for. Near the farmer's house there was a field in grass and that's where all the travellers stayed in their caravans. A lot of them were our relations. We had a bra crack with them all and the singing in the fields was wonderful. Everyone wanted my mother to sing the old songs. I wouldn't sing because I was too shy then. There was one old woman who started to sing a song and I guarantee it lasted one hour and a half. To my recollection it was a gruesome tale about a young girl having her head cut off for loving someone her parents didn't approve of. When we got home that night my mother said to me, 'Sheila did you hear that auld woman's song?'

'Oh my God,' I said, 'aye, but with folk shouting I couldn't hear it all.'

'Well,' said my mother, 'she got her heid cut aff.'

'Aye, I heard that bit.'

'Although her heid was aff, she wouldn't die. I am going up the morn tae get it fae the auld woman.' Next day it was raining and we couldn't pick berries. My father was away with the car, and we had to wait till he came home. It was now three o'clock by the time we got up to Marshalls that day, and the old woman had moved off with her caravan, wandering the country. We never saw her again.

Two days later there was to be a ceilidh up at Marshalls to celebrate the end of the season. When we arrived there, there was a big fire burning and masses of travellers were gathered around it. There were about five kettles on and the farmer had produced eats. We got settled round the fire and an accordion and fiddle began to play a selection of tunes. Some travellers were trying to dance – they were only messing about, but they were enjoying themselves. There was also plenty of beer flowing. My mother was first to sing of course, and it had to be 'The Berry Fields o Blair'. It was a favourite with everybody there.

The night was great until a fight broke out. As is usual with travellers, it was about a lassie going out with a laddie the family didn't approve of. The two families started to fight, so we all piled into the car and went home. On the way down the road, we saw the laddie and lassie running like the blazes to get away from the fighting. We stopped the car and gave them a lift to Blair. Two weeks later we heard they had set up home in a caravan beside her family. They were two weeks living together, so she was soiled and the families had to give in because no other man would look at her. Although the girl's father had initially had to fight for her honour, the families became friends after that. The couple didn't get married, though; they only lived together.

*

Peter Shepard and Jimmy Hutcheson became great friends of my family and it was they that started the Blair Folk Festival that year, the greatest festival in Scotland. What made it so good was that all the last generation of singers were alive then and people came from all over the world to the festival. My family was booked for it, as was the great Jeannie Robertson, auld Willie Scott, Daisy Chapman and Davie Stewart (the Auld Galoot), to mention but a few – there were many more travellers and performers who came to that first festival. I entered the competition that year and won it for singing 'The Twa Brothers'. I got a certificate and a cup donated by Grampian Television. It was wonderful. Thanks to Peter and Jimmy that year, a lot of folk singers stayed with us and my mother was in her element catering for them and having songs and stories in the house every night. I think it was the only time of the year my mother and father could agree and didn't have a cross word between them – much to the family's great relief, I can tell you. My husband Ian MacGregor, Cathie's man Jimmy Higgins, their son Alex and my sister Rena got a job up at the Backwater Dam, which was to create the reservoir and do away with all the farms and cotter houses up at Glen Isla. The day this area was flooded was a sad one for my father because that was the end of his hawking that glen, which had been so good to him in the past. But my parents always maintained that when one door closes, another one opens.

★

My mother learned this song in Ireland from one of the travellers. It brought back many memories to her whenever she sang it.

Cod Liver Oil

I'm a young married man and I'm tired of life,
For years I've been wed to a sickly young wife,
She does nothing all day now, but sit down and cry,
And wishing tae God every day she would die.

So a friend of me own came to see me one day,
And he said that my wife she was pining away,
But if you get a bottle from dear Doctor John,
It's ten unto one that your wife will get strong.

So a bottle, a bottle I bought for to try,
And the way that she drank it you'd swear she was dry,
Another, another she vanished the same
You would swear she had cod liver oil on the brain.

I'm a young married man and I'm tired of life,
For years I've been wed to a sickly young wife,
She does nothing all day now, but sit down and cry,
And wishing tae God every day she would die.

O doctor, dear doctor, oh dear doctor John,
Your cod liver oil is so pure and so strong,
I'm afraid of me life I'll go down in the soil,
If my wife don't stop drinking your cod liver oil.

Now my house it resembles a big chemist shop,
It's covered with bottles from bottom to top,
And in the morning when the kettle does boil,
You would swear it was singing for cod liver oil.

I'm a young married man and I'm tired of life,
For years I've been wed to a sickly young wife,
She does nothing all day now, but sit down and cry,
And wishing tae God every day she would die.

*

One day, my father had to go up Glenshee to pick up some wool
and fleeces. He took my mother with him and on the way up he
asked her if she wanted a shot at driving the car. 'What?' she said.
'After all these years you are now asking me to go behind the
wheel of a car? It's about time. Why did you no teach me lang
before this?'

My father looked at her and said, 'Well, Belle, if I had taught
you earlier, every argument we had, you would have left me and
took the car.' He was dead serious; he really thought that.

Well, she got behind the wheel, and my father told her what

to do. 'Belle,' he said, 'you have watched me driving for years. You should ken what to do by now.'

'Oh,' said my mother, 'I never paid much attention to what you were doing. As long as I got there, I never bothered.' My father just shook his head. So she started it up, put it in gear, and very shakily drove off, stalling it a few times. My father swallowed his temper, and she drove off. After about two hundred yards, she went off the road into a deep ditch. My father had to walk a mile to the first farm to get the farmer to pull the car out of the ditch. I won't repeat what my father said to my mother that day, but she never got the car again to practice on again and they didn't speak for three days, because the exhaust had been torn off the car.

When they arrived home that day, Jimmy, the Highland Chief, my father's cousin, was waiting for my father. 'Well, Bidley,' he said (all the old travellers in those days called my father Bidley because he was a piper and 'biddled' the pipes), 'I have left my wife Brocky. We fell oot and I left her at Dunkeld, and came doon to you for advice. She is in a wee tent in the slate quarries up there.'

'Well,' said my father, 'come on in and Belle will make you a drop o tea.' He had his tea with us that night and my father pitched a wee tent up for him in the back garden. The next morning he came in and had his breakfast. Our breakfast always consisted of either toast and tea or rolls and tea. We didn't believe in cooked breakfasts, it was just the way we were brought up. That morning it was toast and tea.

My father offered him a wee job to do in the old wastins where he kept his rags. 'I have twelve dozen wire sculls to do for this farmer. I beat them till they are straight again then dip them in a bath of silver paint, and it makes them look new. I will pay you if you help me.'

'Oh aye,' said the Chief. 'Thanks Bidley.'

The next morning as my mother was getting up, Brocky was sitting on our step. 'Ah, Belle,' she said. 'The Chief has left me. What am I going to do?'

'Come in', my mother said, 'and I will put the kettle on.' She hurried to the bedroom and told my father Brocky was there. My father jumped out of bed, sneaked out the door, and went round the back for the Chief. He didn't tell him Brocky was there because he wanted it to be a surprise. Well, the Chief came in the back door, and when he saw Brocky he made a dive at her and hugged her, and said he was sorry. They were fine taking their tea, smiling over to one another, but we watched them as they left. She was chasing him up the road with a stick. My father gave him a pound for all the sculls he hadn't done. I'm sure the pound helped them out for food, because the Chief never drank. He carried his Bible with him under his arm, but he couldn't read it – he had never been to school.

*

My husband Ian and I wanted to go back to live in Blair. So Ian went there one night with a crowbar and we squatted in a house in Reform Street. Our kids had loved living in New Alyth, so their father and I weren't very popular. There was Ian my oldest, called after his father, then Hamish, Heather and Gregor.

Not long after we moved, my mother and father bought a house in Yeaman Street, Old Rattray. It was one my mother's brother Donald used to live in. A good while later, my mother got a letter from a woman in Scone, asking her for a particular song my mother knew, 'Dalry'. The woman was Sheila Douglas, the great folklorist. My mother and father went to Scone to visit her and were given a great welcome. Dalry was the name of the place where Sheila's father had come from. She had heard Gus Langlands sing it in a club she ran in Perth, and when she asked him where he got it, he told her it was from Belle Stewart of Blairgowrie. So of course, Sheila wrote to my mother. That was in the early sixties, and we have been great friends ever since. She and her husband Andrew never exploited us in any way. There were plenty of folk that did, but not them. They were sincere from day one, and were, if I may say so, our best friends. Andrew died a few years ago and he is sadly missed.

Dalry

Noo, I'm a saft coun-try chiel and my name's Geor-die Weir. I sup-pose you'll aa won-der what I'm do-in here. But it's just on a vis-it to Gles-ca I've come. For to see a lot of folk I han-nae seen for a lang.

Noo, I'm a saft country chiel and my name's Geordie Weir,
I suppose you'll aa wonder what I'm doin here,
But it's just on a visit tae Glesca I've come,
For to see a lot of folk I hannae seen for a lang.

Noo, I met a wee lassie, but oh, she was shy,
Wi a smile on her lips, and a tear in her eye,
We'd a few drams thegither till the drink took my heid,
Then she stole aa my money; bad scorn tae her breed.

So I wish I was back aince mair in Dalry,
You would ne'er see my face till the day I wid die,
If I only could manage the price o my train,
You wid ne'er see my face back in Glesca again.

Where to sleep the first nicht was a mystery to me,
For I hadnae as much as a crooked bawbee.
Till I met an acquaintance and he didnae grudge,
For tae pay for my bed in a big motel lodge.

And when I got my tea I went oot for a stroll
And I stood at a windae to view a wax doll,
When a wee bloke cam up sayin you'll best dae a slide,
If MacLeod sees your face, he'll soon drag ye inside.

Noo, I wunner what makes aa the folk at me stare,
And ask me tae leave them a lock o my hair,
But I'll lea tae yourself, it is no a hard egg,
When a dog comes and maks a lamppost o yer leg.

When I got under covers, fegs, yon was a fricht,
I may say that my freens had a gie lively nicht,
For it was just like a battlefield on the bedclaes,
Like the Zulus were runnin afore the Scotch Grays.

★

My mother found out one day that my father's cousin Jeannie
Robertson was camped at the Bridge of Ruthven, between
Alyth and Kirriemuir. 'Oh,' said my father, 'we must go and visit.'

So that Sunday, we headed to where Jeannie was camped. We
got a great welcome from her and the family. She had a big pot
of soup on the fire, and a big pot of tatties. We all got soup and
she put a few spoonfuls of tatties in the soup bowl as well. The
soup was delicious; it was made from a ham shank with some
stottin bits she had got from the grocers. We ate our fill and
started to chat around the fire. Jeannie got her photos out and
was passing them round and telling us who everyone was. My
father was handed a photo and he looked at it. 'Jeannie,' he said,
'who took this photo o a pear?' She looked at it.

'That's no a pear Alex, that's my mother'.

Even as I write this, I can still see the shock, horror and shame
on my father's face. Jeannie burst out laughing. Thank God she
saw the funny side of it. 'You are blind, Alex, you will have to go
and get glasses.'

'Aye, so I will,' said my father. We stayed many hours that night
and that is the first time I heard her sing a ballad. From then on
Jeannie was my favourite traveller singer. Sorry mother, but she was.

We visited Jeannie a lot that year. She loved my father's
company, because they shared the same sense of humour, being
cousins. Jeannie never came back after that, because she was too
busy singing and recording for Hamish Henderson, as were we,

Top. (from left) Alex, Belle and Jeannie (Alex's sister),
who is teaching Belle drookerin.

Above. Belle and Sheila

Top. (from left) Rena, Belle, Alex and Sheila

Above. (from left) Alex, Hamish Henderson, Belle, Sheila, Cathie,
John (Cathie's son), Sheila (Cathie's daughter), Diane (Greta's daughter)
and Greta Stewart (daughter of Alex's cousin)

Ian MacGregor and Sheila, just before they were married

Belle and Alex

Top. Big Willie MacPhee, Alex's cousin and best friend

Above. Alex clowning around while on tour in America

Top. (from left) Cathie, Belle, Ian (Sheila's son) and
Sheila at a festival in Lake Como, Italy

Above. Sheila and Belle at a get-together
in Sheila Douglas' house

The Reverend Hamish MacGregor (Sheila's son)

but we always met her at festivals and had a good time.

Wee Jane Turriff was my father's cousin as well and a great singer. We used to go and visit her and her husband Cameron in Mintlaw. Jane sang and accompanied herself on the organ. One day, my mother was sitting beside her near the organ. Jane was taking a mouthful of tea, and whatever my mother said to her, it made the tea fly out of her mouth, and the cup as well, and it spilled all over her organ. Well, my mother went in a panic.

'Never mind, Belle, I have done that often,' Jane assured her. Then they started laughing again. Jane had a good sense of humour. 'Then I dry it oot with my hair-drier. God help us, it was only wanting a mouthful o tea.' My mother sat with the hair-drier for about an hour, drying out the organ, and when she had finished, Jane just began the song again, from the point where she had left off.

*

My uncle Donald died on Christmas Eve, 1964. Just over a week later, on Hogmanay, uncle Andy died. He had gone to join his brother. My mother was devastated to have lost them both. She wrote this song for them:

Song for Donald and Andy

'Twas on a cauld December nicht when fruits and flooers were gone,
My brother Andy left me tae be wi his brother Dan,
The sorrow they have left behind is more than tongue can tell,
I was their only sister and I dearly loved them well.

When I sit and think of days gone by, it makes my heart full sair,
When I think aboot the happy times the three o us had in Blair,
O, I ken I have my bairns, and I have my man and aa,
But never in this wide, wide world were there brothers like you twa.

O, Donald dear I miss ye, for you were sae dear to me,
We loved each other dearly, and we always did agree,
But me and Andy aye fell oot, we were an affa twa,
O please forgive me, Donald, but I miss him maist o aa.

Noo, Jeannie has a gie sere hert, and so does Mary tae,
When they sit and think aboot the things the baith o you did say
And of course there is their bairns, it's hard on them and aa,
But me my life is empty, since I parted wi you twa.

But I hope that God will ease the pain, as weeks and months go by,
For whenever I am by myself my e'en are never dry,
O I ken I'm no the only yin, for you all feel it tae,
But it's grand to ken we'll meet again, on our good Lord's judgment
    day.

                                    *

There was a traveller man who my father always visited and he and
his wife once went pearl-fishing with my parents. My mother and
his wife stayed on the bank of the river near the car. They made a
big fire and put the kettle on. My father and the man went up the
river a bit. 'I'm no putting on waders today,' my father said, 'I am
going to dive for the shells today. I have a pair of Belle's bloomers
I'm going to put on. So he went behind a tree and put on these
big, big bloomers with elastic in the legs. Then he dived down and
came up with two shells. Showing off, he was. The second time he
dived down, the bloomers came off and started to float down the
river. They came to where my mother could see them, and they
just floated past. Up she got and ran to where they were. My father
was shouting to her to get him something to put on.

My mother was reeling mad. 'I gave you my new knickers, and
you have lost them. Get something to wear yourself.' The man

went back to the car and brought my father a pair of trousers.

My mother kept going on about her new knickers. He had to go and buy her another pair, and I went with him. I wished I hadn't. He said to the man in the shop when we went in, 'Have you got a pair of barrage balloons I can buy?'

The man looked at him, and said, 'Excuse me?'

I spoke up then. 'It's knickers he wants for my mother.'

The man smiled, and gave us the knickers. I never went to that shop again.

★

This is another story my father used to tell.

Johnny in the Cradle

There was once a tailor an he travelled the country right around an every place he got an order, he stayed till he made what was ordered. He came tae a wee fairm an he rapped on the door an the man came oot an said, 'Is that you, tailor?'

'Yes,' he says, 'are ye needin onything the day?'

'Oh, yes,' he says, 'I was just goin tae send for ye. I want a suit o clothes made.'

So he went intae the room an he heard a wee bairn greetin. An it was goin, 'Uhuh! Uhuh! Uhuh!' Sore greetin!

'What's wrong wi the bairn?' says the tailor.

'Oh,' he says, 'he's been like that since he was born!'

'What age is he?'

'He's eighteen month old. He gret like that since he was born. We've tae pit him intae anither room tae get sleepin.'

'My goodness, that's terrible,' says the tailor. 'Ach, but he'll no bother me. I'll just make your suit.'

One Friday the fairmer comes in an he says, 'I wonder, tailor, could ye look efter Johnny? I'm awa tae the mairket wi ma wife. He's in the cradle ben the room. Ye can take your stuff ben there.'

'Oh,' he says, 'I'll be aa right. You away tae the market and I'll look efter Johnny.'

When they were away aboot two or three mile doon the road, Johnny stoppit greetin ao a sudden. 'My God,' says the tailor, 'he's stoppit greetin!'

'Aye,' says Johnny, 'I've stoppit greetin aa right. Are they far awa?'

'Oh aye, 'he says, 'they're aboot two or three mile awa.'

'Would ye like a tune?' says Johnny.

'Oh aye,' says the tailor, 'I wad like a tune. What dae ye play?'

'I'll show ye,' he says. He pit his hand intae the cradle and pulled oot a big long straw and he burred hissel oot an he started tae play reels and jigs and marches and the tailor's working away at the suit.

Then Johnny says, 'Wad ye like a dram, tailor?'

'Oh aye,' says the tailor, 'but where are ye goin tae get it?'

An he jumped oot the cradle an went tae the press an blew his breath on the lock, opened the press an took the bottle o whisky an glasses. He gied yin tae the tailor and yin tae himself. Then he says, 'I wonder, are my mother an faither comin hame?'

'Aye,' says the tailor, 'they should be aboot a mile fae hame noo.'

So Johnny pit the whisky awa an pit the straw back in the cradle an startit tae greet again. 'Uhuh! Uhuh! Uhuh!'

So the fairmer comes in an he says, 'Well, tailor, were ye bothered wi Johnny?'

'Not a bit,' says the tailor. 'The best day I ever had!' Johnny's aye watchin him an greetin awa. The tailor waited till the fairmer went oot tae the byre tae milk the kye an he went oot tae him an telt him aboot Johnny playin tunes on straw and giein him a dram.

'Aw,' says the fairmer, 'that cannae be!'

'Well then,' says the tailor, 'next Friday, you say you're gaun tae the mairket, then jist stand in the lobby an ye'll hear him.'

So the next week, the fairmer says tae the tailor, 'Will ye look efter Johnny when we gang tae the mairket?'

'I'll look efter Johnny aa right,' says the tailor. So the fairmer an his wife were supposed tae be away, but they're standin in the lobby.

So Johnny says, 'Are they far away, tailor?'

'Oh aye, they'll be two or three mile doon the road noo,' says the tailor.

'Would ye like a tune again?' he says.

'Oh aye,' he says, 'I'd like a tune.'

So he put his hand underneath an pulled oot this long straw again an he started to play jigs an reels, strathspeys an marches. 'My word!' says the tailor, 'ye can play that thing!'

'Oh aye, I can play it. Would ye like a dram, tailor?'

'Aye, I'd like a dram.'

An he went tae the press again an huffed on the lock an he's oot again wi the whisky an the man an woman nearly took a fit! Then the corn straw's oot again an he's playin an the tailor's dancin!

'Dae ye think they'll be comin back noo?' he says.

'Aye,' says the tailor, 'they cannae be far away.' So he jist pits aa thing back an starts tae greet again, an the tailor's sewin the suit of claes.

The fairmer comes in an he says, 'Ye'll be tired listenin tae Johnny greetin!'

'Oh no,' says the tailor. 'I enjoyed the day fine.'

He went oot tae the byre wi the fairmer later on an says, 'Did ye see him? Did ye hear?'

'I did that,' says the fairmer. 'What can I dae?'

'Now, you leave it tae me,' says the tailor. 'I'll cure him. Get me a griddle an pit some horse manure on top o the griddle.' Then he took the griddle an pit it on the swey in the old-fashioned fireplace an blew the fire up till it was blazin. 'Come on, Johnny, I want you!' he says, an he went owre to tae the cradle. But when Johnny heard that, he's whoosh! Oot o the cradle an up the chimney in a ball o fire. An he cries, 'I wish I'd been langer wi ma mither, I'd hae kent her better!'

Ye can take what meanin ye like oot o that. When the fairmer an his wife lookit in the cradle they found their ain bairn lyin there in place o the changeling the fairies had left.

*

It came round to the Blair festival again. That year we met Kenny Goldstein, who was a collector from America. He and his wife were gems of folk. We didn't know he was a high-up professor in

the States, and we just treated him like anyone else. The last night
of the festival, when it was all over, everyone came back to my
mother's house, 'Lyndhurst', in Yeaman Street. My mother had
named the house after an old pipe tune. There were three rooms
full of people having ceilidhs. The police heard all the noise with
the singing and pipes, so they chapped on the door and my
mother went to the door.

'Oh, it's you, Belle. Having a bit of a party are you?'

'No,' said my mother. 'It is the last night of the folk festival,
and we're having a last ceilidh. Do you want to come in for a
wee while?' They hesitated, but they came in for a time.

'Mind, Belle,' one of them said, 'if we get complaints from the
neighbours you'll have to stop, but I see the neighbours are in
the other room enjoying themselves.' They smiled and left.

Well, that was another year of the festival over. My mother
used to make up poems as well as songs. Here is a poem she
wrote about the Blair festival in 1969.

Blair Festival 1969

The festival has come again,
They say it is the last.
If it is, we still have memories
Of the three that's in the past.
To me this one was very good,
For I really did have fun.
But the main event to me of course
Was the cup that Sheila won.

The ceilidh in our own house
Upon the Saturday night,
There were so many people there,
The house was packed real tight
Maurice Fleming he was there,
The pride above them aa,
It was him that started the Stewarts' fame
In the years that's passed awa.

There was a marvellous ceilidh band.
To hear the rattlin o their drums,
You'd think all hell broke loose.
There were great singers there as well,
Wha fairly did their share;
I will never forget the friends we met
At the festival of Blair.

The council was upset again
With litter on the street,
But I ken a far mair dirtier thing
They've trampt below their feet,
Just take your dirty linen:
Though you bleach it on the green,
Wi all your new detergents,
You couldna wash it clean.

Cathie had a party, upon the Monday night
The Galoot came in wi dark glasses on
And he couldna see the light.
There was Willie Scot and Daisy,
They were a handsome pair;
They came tae Blair for the festival
And fairly did their share.

To me it was delightful,
It was a grand affair
I think it was the best yin yet,
This festival o Blair.

The Blairgowrie festival eventually moved from Blairgowrie to
Kinross. It was still a wonderful festival. We went every year to
support it and were booked to perform, of course. At the last
festival in Blair, my father played a joke on the others. He got
dressed up in women's clothes, put on one of mother's fur coats,
a wig and a head square. Then he headed for the town hall. In he
went, and what a sight he was. He said to the steward, in a

woman's voice, 'I have come to enter the competition for singing.' The steward went in with a very red face to tell the organiser. The organiser came out and looked at my father and said, 'I hear you want to enter the competition.'

He kept his head down and said, 'Yes I do.'

Well, what could the organiser do except usher him into the hall? 'What's your name, madam?'

He answered, 'Blind Mag.' So the organiser filled in the form and put his name down as Blind Mag.

When his name was called, he went up on the stage and started to strip off his wig and the clothes. The hall was in hysterics; everyone laughed and laughed. My mother, Cathie and I hadn't recognised him either. My father was the star act that year. But he never won the trophy for singing.

★

My brother John was down in Hatfield for a time and he wanted Ian and me and Cathie and her husband Jimmy to come down as there was plenty of work at a building site. So we headed south. We bought a small caravan and stayed in Colney Heath, not far from Hatfield. My husband Ian and Cathie's man Jimmy walked about three miles every morning to their work. Then we moved into Hatfield, to the site of the tower block they were building, and it was great because we were living right beside their work. Cathie got a flat at Rodney Court in Hatfield. It wasn't long till my mother and father came down as well and stayed with Cathie.

One day a man came to Cathie's door, a wee Austrian he was, and asked for the Stewart family. He was a researcher for Ewan MacColl. How he had heard we were there was a mystery, but we took him in and waited to see what he had to say. He stayed with Cathie for a few days then left to go back to London. He asked if it was alright for Ewan to visit us there. We said, yes, of course.

So a week later, Ewan arrived with John Brune – that was the wee Austrian's name. We didn't know at this time that Ewan, who was Scottish, was such a famous man down south. We fairly took to him and his wife – they were great folk. We recorded many of the old ballads for him and we used to travel from Hatfield to London to visit them. It was a grand time for us, and, I hope, for them as well. This is a song my mother wrote then.

The Stewart Family

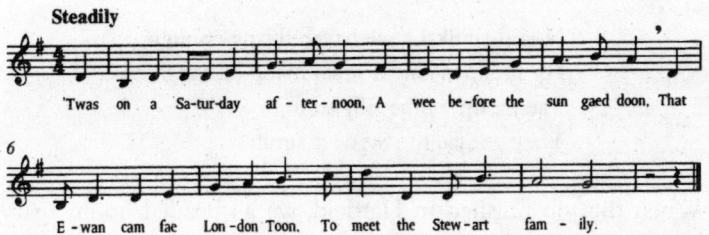

'Twas on a Sa-tur-day af-ter-noon, A wee be-fore the sun gaed doon, That E-wan cam fae Lon-don Toon, To meet the Stew-art fam-ily.

'Twas on a Saturday afternoon,
A wee before the sun gaed doon,
That Ewan cam fae London Toon,
To meet the Stewart family.

When he came in we were gey shy,
But we got acquainted as time gaed by,
And afore he left, you could hear him cry,
'You are a helluva family.'

Now to me his wife was awfa nice,
For she gave me some o her advice,
To never dae the same thing twice,
For it might upset the family.

So noo ye ken them awfa weel,
And him he is an honest chiel,
We've telt him tales that wid fear the deil,
That terrible Stewart family.

Noo we've had mony a happy nicht,
And whiles my e'en were awfa ticht,

But Bessie sees that we're aa richt,
By feedin the Stewart family.

Then as we aa gaed ben the room,
And we aa got sittin doon,
We had a dram tae keep in tune,
Me and the Stewart family.

Noo, I think I have havered lang enough,
For the man and woman maun be tough,
Tae pit up wi the silly stuff
They got fae the Stewart family.

When the job finished in Hatfield, we all headed home again, back to Blair.

All was quiet for a while until we got a letter from Ewan asking us to come down to London and appear at his club, the Singers' Club. We were excited about it, but it did mean we had to drive down to London, which, from the milestone outside our house, we knew was 500 miles away. A week later, we got the car ready. It was an old Vauxhall, but a good runner. We then headed to London and performed at the club. On the way back we performed at a club in Nottingham. A great friend of ours, Gil Harper, stayed just outside Nottingham. My mother called him her adopted son, so I guess he was my adopted brother, and still is. He is a wonderful guitarist and a singer as well. We stayed with Gil's mother for a few days, then came home again. The money we got then for performing was twenty pounds – five pounds each.

*

We settled down again and my mother and father continued hawking. Well, my father did. My mother went with him but stayed sitting in the car. He asked Cathie and me to go with them one day and help him put out some bills asking for rags and scrap. So we went with him up to Pitlochry. It was a great place to hawk. We had a lorry with us that day, and coming home to Blair by the back road, near Butterstone, we met the Highland Chief and Brocky.

This was the first time we had seen them since that time they had separated. My father pulled up the lorry and asked them where they were going. The Chief said he was going two miles up the glen. So my father said, 'Jump in the back of the lorry and we will give you a lift up.' So they climbed up into the lorry and we drove the two miles they had to go, and the Chief tapped on the back window to tell my father to stop. My father pulled up and got out of the cab and Jimmy the Chief jumped down, but Brocky was too scared. My mother tried to encourage her, as did Cathie and I. Jimmy was shouting, 'Jump woman, jump! I will catch you, I'll no let you faa!' So she jumped right on top of his chest, and knocked him over the bank with her on top of him. They rolled and rolled down to the bottom of the hill.

My father shouted, 'Are you all right, Jimmy?'

'I think so Bidley, but I dinnae ken aboot her.'

'I am okay as well, Bidley, I'm havin a sloosh.'

'God pity that woman, she is moich. Ye ken she'll be the death of me yet. Thanks Bidley and Belle, see you again some time soon I hope!' the Chief called up to us.

When we got home, my brother said the Radiogramme was looking for my father and mother, and that his wife Lizzie was with him. He and Lizzie had a wee lassie and one son. Her mother was watching the bairns for them and they were camped at the Sugar and Tea Old Road, near Kirriemuir. What the Radiogramme's real name was I don't know, but travellers are always giving nicknames to folk – then we ken who we're speaking about. He didn't mind us calling him the Radiogramme. In fact, he was chuffed, but it was only us who called him that. He called my father 'Elec' and my mother Bie.

Somebody from the town had come to them the night before, driven them out of their tent and put fire to it. Everything belonging to them was broken. They had managed to get a lift through to ask my mother and father if they had an old tent they could give them. 'Well, the tent I have', said my father, 'is a bell tent. I don't have a cover to make a bow tent, but we will take you hame and put up the tent for you if you like.'

'That wid be grand,' said the Radiogramme.

My mother and father took them back home and my mother gave Lizzie dishes, pots and blankets to help them out.

★

A few nights later, Hamish Henderson arrived. He wanted to meet old Charlotte Higgins and her husband Jocky. They were Cathie's man Jimmy's parents and were two good singers. My mother was always up for visitors, especially when there was singing on the go. She loved people even more as she got older, and she was a great hostess; everyone was made to feel welcome. That night, old Charlotte and Jocky came up, and this was the first time I heard this song:

Green Grows the Laurel

> Green grows the laurel, soft falls the dew,
> Happy was I when I parted from you,
> But by our next meeting I hope you'll prove true,
> We'll share the green laurels and violets so blue.
>
> He passes my window both early and late,
> And the look that he gives me it makes my heart break.
> And the look that he gives me ten thousand times o'er,
> I said here is the young man I once did adore.
>
> Green grows the laurel, soft falls the dew,
> Sorry was I when I parted from you,
> But by our next meeting I hope you'll prove true,
> We'll share the green laurels and violets so blue.
>
> He wrote me a letter in sweet rosie lines,
> I wrote him an answer all twisted and twined,
> Saying, keep your love letters and I will keep mine,
> You write to your sweetheart, and I'll write to mine.

Green grows the laurel, soft falls the dew,
Sorry was I when I parted from you,
But by our next meeting I hope you'll prove true,
We'll share the green laurels and violets so blue.

This is a song that I only heard old Charlotte Higgins sing. Now you hear it sometimes in the folk clubs, but not very often. Jocky also sang a song but I never learned it, except for a few lines – I remember something like:

In a garden a lady walking,
Till one fine stranger came passing by.

I don't know any more of it, but my mother and I were so into ballads that I just had to mention it. These small fragments had an awful power to me and my mother, reminding us of a bygone age. Another one my mother taught me was from her uncle, Hendry MacGregor:

Dukes and Earls

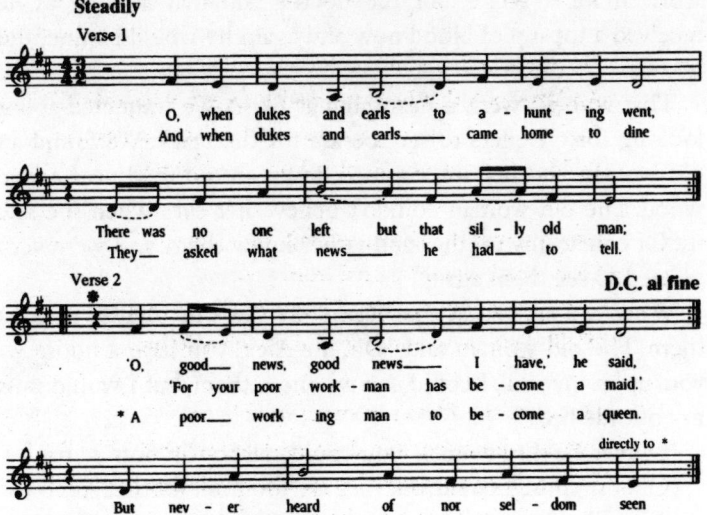

O, when dukes and earls to a-hunting went,
There was no one left but that silly old man;
And when dukes and earls came home to dine
They asked what news he had to tell.

'O, good news, good news I have,' he said,
'For your poor workman has become a maid.'
But never heard of nor seldom seen
A poor working man to become a queen.

These kinds of ballads are not sung often enough today. My mother thought this as well. As the last of my line, I don't want them forgotten, but of course they will be eventually.

★

Around that time, my father wasn't feeling too well so my mother got the doctor up to see him. His white blood cells were eating up his red blood cells, and he had to go in for blood transfusions. Once he got them, he was fine. My mother was worried for a while, but the doctor said that as long as he received a top-up of blood now and again he would be fine, and he was.

That year we went up camping at Elgin. We wandered about looking for travellers to stay beside for the crack. We found an old woman and her son camped down an old road near a wee wood. The old woman couldn't believe her eyes when she saw us. Of course, my mother and father knew them, and were very pleased to see them again.

When we arrived at their camp we put our caravan next to them. The old woman said, 'Oh, me Alex, you have a hoose wi you, upon my soul. I could dae wi one o them, but I would miss my outside fire.'

'Dinnae be silly, woman, you could still hae an outside fire.'

'Oh, I suppose I could, but they are too posh for the likes o us.'

'Awa, silly woman, I am just the same as you – a traveller.'

'Aye, but you have moved on to modern times. I am still stuck

wi the auld ways. Well, anyway,' said the old woman, 'the kettle
has just boiled. Have a cup o slab wi us.'

We all gathered round the fire while the old woman made the
tea. We watched her son who was busy feeding the fire with silk
stockings out of a bag he had.

'What you daen, Robin, wi the stockins?' we asked him.

'Well,' he said, 'under them is a fish I caught this morning, and
I am cookin it.'

'God bless me,' said my father, 'it will taste like cloots.'

'I'm no heedin aboot that, as lang as I fill my belly.'

We watched him take it out, raking it with a stick. He lifted it,
and it was too hot. 'Gods curse you, fish, I've burned my hand wi
you, you adulterated flattrin!' He waited till it was a bit cooler
this time, tried to rake it on the grass to clean it then ate it. I
think he ate more grass and silk stockings than the fish.

'Upon my soul, that was good,' he said, 'but I forgot to put salt
on it.' So he licked a wee drop of salt off his hand.

'That's better,' he said.

'Awa silly laddie,' said the old woman. 'Ye ken, Alex, he's no aa
there.'

'Where am I then?'

'Oh, shut up, fool, we have visitors.'

We thought they had no food, because of the fish thing, but in
fact they had plenty. He had just wanted to cook it for himself.

The old woman played the chanter for a bit – my father didn't
have his pipes with him. She wasn't a great piper, but she wasn't
bad. 'I am getting oot o breath now,' she said 'and it's harder tae
blaw, but I love it.' The laddie started to dance to her playing the
chanter. He wasn't really dancing, but he was enjoying it. We all
were – they were great company.

Nobody in this whole world, except a traveller, knows that to
get speaking to another old traveller like that gives you a
satisfaction you can't describe. It was wonderful.

When we came home, there was a letter waiting for my mother,
asking my father and her to go to America for a tour. 'Maybe
you won't be able to go Alex, wi your blood,' she told my father.

'No, I'll be fine. I will ask the doctor for a top-up before I go'.

So he did and he was fine. They were very excited about going. While they were away, my mother phoned us often and told us how much they were enjoying it. They got a good welcome from the Americans and they already knew some of the people there, because they had come to the Blair festival. It was a little too hot for them, they said, but otherwise it was great.

They were supposed to stay two weeks, but in the end the organisers kept them there for a month. When they returned, they were both glowing. My father had to go into hospital again for another top-up, but he was fine after a few days.

*

This is a story my uncle John, my father's brother, told us. My mother liked it, so now I tell it to you.

The Face

Round about 1939, I went into the RAF and I was stationed at a camp in England. I was granted my first leave and I dashed to the train in a hurry to get home. I didn't have a lot of money, as I was trying to save it, for I had a good long stop in Edinburgh and I wanted to keep it, no for an English drink, but for a Scottish drink. So the train rumbled on till I finally arrived in Edinburgh. I was headed for Montrose, and had an hour to wait, so I came up and ontae the street. It was the time o the blackout, and I didn't know if I was in Princes Street or no – I had only been in Edinburgh twice before. I went into some pubs, and I had a half pint here, and a half pint there, just to pass the time till my train. I was going into this pub when I bumped into a woman in the dim light.

She said, 'Hello John.' She was a young woman of about twenty-one or twenty-two.

'Hello,' I said, 'I don't know you.'

'Come in here where the light is and you will see me better.'

So I did, but I never knew her fae Adam.

'I'm Jean Stewart,' she said finally. 'I'm a cousin of yours.'

She mentions this body and that body in the family. 'Fair enough,' I said. I realised then that I had spoken so long wi her, even if I ran, I would miss my train. So I told her I would have to go and look for a bed for the night.

'That's alright, come tae my hoose, and you can spend the night.'

'Where do you stay?' I asked her. I couldna tell you where she took me – through back streets, doon alleyways, until we came to an outside stair, then an inside stair, and finally an attic room, where she lived. It was a lovely big room, wi the fire blazin in the grate. It looked fine and comfortable. She said, 'Just sit doon there and I will go for something for the tea. Do you want fish?'

'No,' I said, 'I have just had a fish supper, before I met you.'

'Well,' she said, 'I know a wine shop just doon the road, I might get two or three bottles o beer aff him and he's no bad, maybe I can get a half bottle o whisky tae.'

I put my hand in my pocket, and I think it was a fiver I gave her.

'Just take your jacket off and hang it on the back o the chair. I won't be minutes. Or you can go to bed if you like,' she said.

It was one of yon boxed-in beds. 'Where are you going to lie?' I asked.

'In the bed,' she said.

'I couldn't do that,' I said, 'I'll sit on the chair all night.'

'Dae what I'm telling you,' she said, 'go to bed.'

When she said that in that tone, I felt aa queer and I couldn't stop thinking o my wife Maggie. I waited till she went oot, then I took my claes off and I looked at the bed. When we were young, my father made us sleep wi nae shirts on, in case we picked up lice in a strange bed. He was a clean kind o man, my father. So I took my troosers, shoes and shirt and put them under my pillow, and then I got intae the lovely clean sheets. I lay smokin for about five minutes, waitin for her to come back wi the half bottle, when I heard a rattle at the back o a picture that was on the wall. The whole picture slid doon and there was a man's face, with a beard and a skean dhu in his hand! He leans through and says, 'I'll learn you tae lie in my wife's bed,' and he made a lunge at me.

I threw myself oot o the bed, naked, and I could hear the knife go crunch into the bed. Oh boy, I'm oot the door and doon the wooden stairs, doon the outside stairs. I thought he was right at my back. You can think very quickly when you're in a situation like that. So I ran doon a cobbled close till I came to a brae, and in front o me I could see flashlights. Who was this but two police men wi their square lamps like bull's eyes in front o their belts. 'What's wrong, what's wrong, what's wrong?' they asked.

'A man up that stair made a dive at me wi a knife,' I told them.

'Where aboots was it?' they asked me. My teeth were chitterin. It was gie cold at twelve o'clock at night, and I was naked.

'Come on back wi us, and we will get your clothes.'

But could I find that house again? I tried every stair and every close, but they all looked the same, and wi the fright I had ran further than I thought. I heard one of the policeman say to the other, 'I think he's a bloody loony.'

'We'll just run him in.'

'You'll no run me in boy,' I says and I take off down the close. The police were blowin their whistles at me and I ran doon the close and on to another road till I came to a fence. I jumped over it and made off like a hare, and wi me being barefoot and naked I was liftin lumps oot o the grun. I was like a whippet! I heard the crowd behind me, and it faded and faded as I climbed this sleepered fence, and jumped awa doon the other side. Oh my feet! It was a railway line, and I was jumping from sleeper to sleeper on my bare feet. 'I hope a train doesn't come,' I said to myself. I didn't know it at the time but it was the Forth Bridge I was on and I could see the water on each side. By this time it was kinda breakin daylight. 'If I'm caught naked,' I said to myself, 'I'll get the jail.'

It was the back end of the year, and it was getting kind o frosty. I searched that field to see if there was a scarecrow and I saw one on the skyline, so I went right over to it, but all it had on was an auld busted hat – nae jacket, nae troosers. So I took the hat, thinking it would keep my head warm anyway. I stuck the hat on and came back to the road and up round the corner, and I looked across the field, and I saw a wee peep o light. I wondered if there was anybody in that hoose. I made for it and hid in a blackthorn bush beside it.

It was getting lighter, and lighter. I saw a man and a woman come oot the door, and they stood talking. Now, I thought to myself, if I could get that man to look, I could give him a wave, and explain to him, but instead of him looking it was her. She turned to him, and I suppose she said, 'A naked man!' They turned to go back in the door when I shouted to them. I thought, I'll make a kirk or a mill o it, but the two o them went into the hoose and then there was about twenty came back oot, and they looked at me, and ran as if the devil was efter them across the field. I went into the house and found clothes and headed for Montrose, hopefully never to see Edinburgh again.

*

It was a great thing when my mother got the BEM from the queen, but not everyone in Blair thought so. She was once standing in a queue at one of the shops in Blair, when a woman behind her tapped her on the shoulder, and said, 'Why should you, a tink, get a medal from the queen? There are more deserving people needing it more than you.'

My mother stared her in the eye and said, 'Ask her Majesty.'

When she came home, she was shaking, not with shame but with anger. She would never have argued in the shop and disgraced herself, but I think that's what the woman wanted. No matter what we achieved in the folk scene, we tried to keep our heads above water – but not by changing, because we stayed true to our culture and our heritage. Some people in Blair long ago acted as if we weren't even human, but I hope they have reproached themselves and perhaps think of us in a better light now. It's just a pity my mother and father missed out on the acceptance I receive now. Belle Stewart was the greatest person that ever came out of Blair.

She loved Blairgowrie and Rattray, despite what she suffered here. She used to say, 'Sheila, no matter where we were on this earth, as long as we said we were travellers it would just be the same. They would send a telegram to the moon to warn them we were coming.' She had a good sense of humour my mother, but she never let country hantle bother her.

My mother had another great saying. 'If I was cremated, and the highest person in the land was cremated, and the ashes were put in jars in a room, could anybody pick my jar from theirs?'

Well, what can you say to that? She had an answer for everything. My husband Ian used to call her 'Regal Belle'.

She suffered a lot in her life, but nothing could bring her down. She was never happier than when she was surrounded by folk singers, who took us as we were. I remember once we did a gig in a blind school in London, and a man came up to us as we arrived. 'Are you the tinkers?' he asked, 'because if you're not, you're not welcome here.' It felt wonderful to be wanted by them for who we were.

★

That year we went up by Oban and stayed on the Ganavan Sands with our trailers. There were myself and my family, Cathie and her family and my parents. We all went to the town for groceries the day after we arrived and during this time, Cathie lost her son John. We searched for him everywhere but couldn't find him. A woman saw us in a panic and said to us, 'I just saw a wee boy over at the boats.'

Well, we charged over, and there he was speaking to the fisherman who had just landed his catch. 'What a great wee boy you have there. Real chatty. He has earned you your tea for tonight.'

'I hope', Cathie said, 'he did not ask you for fish.'

'No,' said the man, 'he just said he liked fish.' He winked at Cathie.

He gave us a bucket of white fish, and my father and everyone else had a great time cleaning and sorting them for the pan. One thing we woman could do in my family was to prepare food – gut and clean fish, pluck chickens, skin a rabbit. We had been brought up learning how to do it.

It rained all the next day in Oban. My mother woke up with a sore throat. 'Oh, Alex,' she said, 'I wish I had something to sook for this sore throat o mine.'

My father not being very polite said, 'I'll gie you something to sook the noo if you dinnae shut up Belle. You would think you were the only woman that ever had a sore throat.'

But of course he went to the chemist and got tablets for her, just to keep her quiet.

My father decided to get his pipes oot to play the main street of Oban. He played for an hour and got forty-five pounds. When he came home to the trailers, he said to my mother, 'No bad, Belle, eh?'

'That's great Alex, it's better than the pearl-fishing, and your no in the cold weather all day.'

We went home next day, and my father's cousin, Big Willie MacPhee, came over to see him. 'Alex,' he said, 'what do you think of going up the glen in the summer piping to the tourists?' Now, my father remembered about Oban and he told Willie about it. 'We could go to Glen Coe and try there.' There wasn't much left o the summer, but they decided to go up for a week and try it. There were too many pipers there already, but all the same, they came back with two hundred pounds. It was sore on the back standing all day playing pipes, but they managed it.

So, from then on, Big Willie and my father went piping every year. Of course my mother and Willie's wife Bella went with them too. They found a special place to play, where there were no other pipers: Loch Lochy, which is on the road between Fort William and Inverness, near the Seven Heads of Glengarry, where they used to go and shop sometimes.

The second year they were there, my mother and Bella decided they would sell white heather, so they went to a nursery past Crieff and bought some. They bought some kitchen foil and made wee bunches, wrapping the stocks with the silver foil – they looked lovely. My mother and Bella made a lot of money, which they shared, and of course they were allowed to keep that money. Days had changed since my father would have kept everything, but of course he used to make all the money back then and not my mother.

The tourist buses were coming in thick and fast, and the money was pouring in too. My father of course had to go for his top-ups at the hospital every so often, but Willie piped by himself till my father was able to come back. My father and Willie were cousins, but they were also best friends. The real bond started when they were piping together, and then, of course, my mother and Bella became close as well. There were also other travellers down the road a bit in a lay-by, making and selling baskets, and they became good friends to them as well. They would go there at nights and have a good old crack with them to pass the time. There was also a roadman who stayed in a cottage nearby and he looked after that stretch of road. He was the nicest wee man you could possibly meet. He lived alone as his wife had died a few years previously, and he was lonely. One day, Bella would feed him and the next day my mother would feed him. They became very attached to him and he looked forward every year to my mother, my father, Willie and Bella arriving. They spent many good nights at a hotel near to where they piped called Letterfinley. They got to know the owners pretty well and also became great friends with them.

One year, my father decided he would take my two sons, Ian and Hamish, to pipe at another lay-by. Ian was fifteen, and Hamish was fourteen. I drove them there with their pipes – it was only about 500 yards away from where my father and Willie piped. But when we arrived, Ian wouldn't even get out of the car. So Hamish stood at this lay-by on his own while I went back to my father to tell him Ian wouldn't get out of the car because he was too shy. I looked down the road and there was Hamish wandering back. He was too ashamed as well, so that idea was out the window.

My father took my daughter and her cousin, my brother Andy's daughter Maureen, to dance to the tourists while they played. It was a great success that year, but later the girls wanted to do girly things, and so they didn't go back up there again.

Not far from where they lived on the lay-by was a caravan site for tourists. The man who owned it asked my father and Willie if they would come and play the pipes one night. When they arrived, there were about a dozen folk in a hall on the site. Ten minutes later the hall began to fill up, until there were about 150 people there. My father said to my mother, 'Belle, this is going to be bigger than I thought. You will have to sing here. We will make it into a ceilidh dance.' My mother didn't always agree with my father, but this time she did. She began singing. After two songs, a woman came up to her and asked, 'Are you Belle Stewart, from Blair?'

'Yes,' said my mother, 'I am.'

'Oh my goodness,' she said, 'you are my husband's favourite singer, and he isn't here tonight. He will be hopping mad because he missed you. We come from the Seven Heads.' My mother realised then that there were folk from the glen there that night, as well as the tourists. 'Where are you staying?' the woman asked.

'Down at Loch Lochy lay-by – you know, the twin lay-by at each side of the road.'

'I know it well,' said the woman. 'Can I bring my husband tomorrow to see you there?'

'Of course you can,' said my mother. Next day about two o'clock the woman arrived with her husband, who was in a wheelchair. He was so excited to see my mother. He had brought her a bunch of roses and a box of chocolates. My mother made them tea and biscuits and they had a good time speaking about songs. 'My favourite song you sing, Belle, is "The Bonnie Hoose o Airlie",' he said. So my mother sang it to him, and he was over the moon. She was happy to please the poor soul.

Two days later a car pulled up at the caravan. It was the same woman, but she was alone. She knocked on the door, and my mother answered. 'Belle,' she said, 'my Norman died last night, very peacefully in his sleep. He had cancer you know.' My mother was stunned by the news, and didn't know what to say to the woman. 'I came to tell you, Belle, you made his last day on earth a very happy one. He spoke about it all the way home, and the icing on the cake was when you sang his favourite song.'

My mother was choked up. 'Well, I must go now, Belle, and see to things, but I will never forget the pleasure you gave my man. Goodbye then, Belle.' She hugged my mother, jumped into her car and left.

That night was a sad night for my mother and my father knew it. He asked Willie and Bella to come into his trailer to try and cheer her up. So in they came after their tea, and as they were sitting cracking, my mother told them about the old man. My father wanted to get off the subject because he could see it was depressing her. So he began to tell a story. My mother loved stories, so she was all ears.

The Black Dog of the Stewarts

My father Jock Stewart was comin home one night, and it was a clear moonlit night in Aberdeenshire. There was a wee fence beside a rickle o a wall and as he was walkin along, this big black dog jumped right up on top o the fence. It jumped that close to my father's face, he shouted, 'Shoo! Shoo! Shoo!' He put his hand over the fence, down to the dog, and his hand went right through it as if it wasn't there. Now, my father had told us this often, and my father is dead now and I wouldn't tell you a lie.

Once when we were in Ireland, my brother John and I had a dog, and that dog would have fought wi the devil himself. It was a vicious dog, and moich, and it would fight wi any dog, and tear its entrails oot, but it was a good hunter. John also had another big dog he called Fry, and he could race. Now, we were oot in the moonlight poachin. In Ireland there are no poachin laws. You can wander any place and hunt and poach as you want, as long as you don't cause any damage. We were in this field, and there were clumps of bushes, and the moon was that bright the frost was glittery. You could see for miles. Wir dogs were sensin something, they were hot on the trail round about us, and just like that there was a big black retriever dog, with curls round it. You could even see the moon through the curls. I could see a glitter o a belt round its neck, and it was standing as stiff as a poker. Wir dogs were scentin back and forth and up and doon, and never noticed that dog. Now somethin made us run – we thought it was the gamekeeper comin, and we arrived back onto the road. It was after we were away we thought about it. How did wir dogs no even growl at it and pay no attention to it at all? Then we remembered about the black dog that follows the Stewarts. It doesn't mean anything to me, unless they sold their soul to the devil or somethin like that, years and years ago. I remember my father sayin there was a black dog follows the Stewarts and they were supposed to see it three times.

There was another time I saw a dog. That was between Kirriemuir and Forfar. There used to be a railway crossin there and some people were killed at this crossin. As you passed that, there were two buildings on the right-hand side of the road. You pass that, and you go around a corner, and down a long hill. I was comin back up this hill one day, and this dog came right oot on the road and seemed to get right in front o my car. I never felt as if I ran over anythin, and when I looked back there was nothing there.

My mother felt a little better. The story had lifted her spirits a wee bit. Big Willie asked her to sing 'The Maid of Kilmore'. He liked that song. So my mother sang it to him, but you could see her heart wasn't in it.

★

The piping season was over for that year, so my mother and father came home, with a good few pounds in their pockets. We had a booking up in Aberdeen, and Jeannie was to be there as well. On the way up to Aberdeen we saw a man hitchhiking, so my father stopped to give him a lift. The man was about forty years old and well-dressed, wearing a suit and tie. He had red hair and said his name was John Blair. But when we got talking, he sounded to us like a traveller. Cathie and I looked at each other and shook our heads. We listened to him for a long time, blethering away, until my mother looked at him and spoke to him in cant. He answered her in cant. 'Oh my God,' he said, 'you tricked me.'

My mother said to him, 'We kent fine you were a naken, but we let you blether on. Now, your name is not John Blair, is it?'

'No, it's not,' said the man. 'Oh, it's John alright, but no Blair. I just made that up. It's Whyte, and you see,' he said, 'my wife's brothers are looking for me, because I am going to Aberdeen to meet this other woman who I met at the tatties in Crieff. Her name is Maggy Spencer. You won't tell anyone you saw me, will you?'

'No,' said my father. 'It's none of our business really. Your secret is safe with us.' Cathie and I couldn't help but give a wee giggle —what a fankle he'd got himself in.

★

When my mother, Cathie and I started to perform on stage, my mother was the holder of all the songs. I knew them all because of my uncle Donald, but Cathie only knew one or two. We made her learn some more, and she got permission from my mother to sing the ones she knew, but it was more difficult for my mother to sort out mine, as I knew them all. She finally managed it. We all had our own songs and we weren't allowed to dip into each other's. That's the way it was; my mother was the boss of what we could sing on stage. One of Cathie's songs was called 'The Nobleman':

The Nobleman

> A nobleman lived in a mansion
> And he courted his own servant maid
> 'Twas neither for love nor for money
> But only to lead her astray.
>
> One night as he entered her bedroom
> As Mary was loosing her stays,
> ''Tis many fine presents I'll give you
> One night for to lie by your side.'
>
> 'Oh, master, I wonder to hear you,
> A man of such honour and pride,
> To ask a poor innocent lassie
> One night for to lie by your side.

'For if I were to fall with a baby,
'Twould be the very first thing you'd deny,
And me and my baby would perish
And you in your mansion would lie.'

'Now if you were to fall with a baby,
'Twould be the very first thing I would do.
I would write out a cheque for some money
And build a fine cottage for you.'

But he saw that he couldn't get round her,
So he said he would make her his bride,
So now she's a nobleman's lady
And lies by a nobleman's side.

★

We were booked again to go down south and do various clubs.
Once we went to Sidmouth, away near Exeter – far, far down in
England. We were walking along the promenade one day when we
saw some new-age travellers selling jewellery. We had never met
any new-agers before, so we went over to talk to them. They never
washed, they had matted hair, and their dress was not becoming.
We asked them who they were, and they said, 'We are travellers.'

My mother being my mother, said to them, 'No, you're not.'

The man with the matted hair looked at my mother, and said,
'We are, and how would you know anyway?'

'Because we are,' said my mother.

'You are?' said the man. 'But you're dressed too fine to be
travellers.'

'Aye, maybe so,' said my mother. 'Have you ever seen other
travellers with matted hair, like yours, and no washin themselves?'

'Well, no,' he said. He shouted for his wife to come and meet
us, and a few others turned up.

'Maybe we will start a new trend among your travellers,' one
of them said.

'Not on your nelly,' my mother replied, and walked away.

★

Cathie's man Jimmy Higgins went up north to work and arrived at the site where he would be living in a caravan. There were many caravans there for the workers and a big hut with cooking facilities where they ate. Jimmy started work the next day, and he was put with a squad of six. They went to their work and Jimmy began talking to a man who spoke half-broken Irish. They chatted all day. When they got back to their trailers, the man asked Jimmy where he came from and what his name was. So Jimmy said, 'My name is Jimmy Higgins, and I come from Blairgowrie.'

The man stood stock still and looked at him. 'Well, my name is Jimmy Veesy.'

Now, Jimmy knew all about Jimmy Veesy and my mother. They shook hands and Jimmy said, 'Belle Stewart is my mother-in-law.' Jimmy Veesy had to sit down, hearing this after all these years. The wind went out of his sails for a wee while. He said fate had sent Jimmy to him. Then he asked, 'How is Belle, what is she up to? Is she well, is she happy? Tell me all about her.' So he got all the crack from Jimmy about my mother. Jimmy said there was a dreamy look in his eyes, and a tear.

Then he said to Jimmy, 'I made a song up for Belle, would you give it to her when you go back hame? Tell her it's from me, but don't let her husband know.'

So when Jimmy's work finished he came back home. He gave my mother the song, and told her the whole story. There was more than a tear in her eye that day. My father was away hawking, so she was relieved and she asked him the same questions about Jimmy Veesy that Jimmy Veesy had asked about her. She read the song and said to Cathie, 'You'll have to say Jimmy took it home for you, fae a man he worked with, and you must learn it and add it to the songs I gave you, and sing it. I must learn it too, though, and sing it as well.'

Don't get me wrong. My mother loved my father, but not the way a wife should. Her one love was Jimmy Veesy. Now when I look back, I realise it must have been terrible for her, never getting the man she truly loved. On the other hand, if she hadn't gone back to my father, I wouldn't be here now to write her biography. My father had had his moments with other women as well when they were separated, but nothing serious, luckily – there were no lassies chapping at the door with a bairn in their arms, thank God.

Cathie learned the song, and so did my mother, and I did as well. I now put it in this book for all to see, and if you knew my mother, you'd see it is a great love song. The Hatton Woods he speaks about in the song are here, in Old Rattray.

Hatton Woods

Kind comrades an companions, and all ye females dear,
To my sad lamentation, I'll pray you lend an ear.
For once I lo'ed a bonnie lass, an to me she proved untrue,
And I left her doon by Hatton woods, my folly for tae rue.

I courted wi this bonnie lass a twelvemonth an a day,
Sometimes among the green grass, sometimes among the hay.
I courted her the lee-lang nicht and part o the next day,
Till she said, 'My dearest Sandy lad, it's time you were away.'

I said, 'My dearest Molly lass, when will ye set a time
When you an I'll get married an hands together jine?
Ye'll sit in yon wee cotter hoose and either spin or shew
While your ain guid-hairted Sandy lad goes whistlin at the ploo.'

Noo, there's Cadum and there's Cadum Mills and Luther Mills likewise
There are woods and waters many, unseen unto your eyes,
But the bonnie woods o Hatton, they aa grow green in May,
It was there about the lassie lived that stole my heart away.

But blessings on yon bonnie lass, wherever she may be,
I wish no evil unto her although she slighted me,
I only wish that she may say some time before she dee,
'Oh, I wish I'd wed yon ploughman lad that sang so sweet to me.'

★

We were getting a good lot of bookings, but not many were in
Scotland. My mother and father went again to America, where the
folk appreciated them. Their favourite place was Boston. They loved
it there, and Boston loved them. My mother and father always used
to joke about on stage, insulting each other. One night at a concert
in New York, my mother as usual slagged off my father, and him her.
At the end of the concert, four women came up to her and said it
was terrible, laying into her husband in public. My mother said to
the, 'It wasn't real, we were only kidding for the audience's sake.'

'Are you sure?' asked one of the women.

'Of course,' said my mother. The woman apologised, and said
she was sorry. Then she asked my mother whether they would
perform at a house party for them the next night.

'Of course,' said my mother, so they went the next night to the
house party in a big mansion. There were 150 guests there. They
had a whip-round for them, and got 500 dollars. My mother
couldn't believe it. She said to my father, 'I must fall out with the
Americans more often!' They both laughed their heads off.

They had a few days free before their next gig and they
relaxed in style. 'I wonder what the Highland Chief and Brocky
would make of this,' said my father. 'God bless them. I would
rather have their crack, than the country hantle's crack.'

'Aye, me tae,' said my mother. My parents were always true to
travellers. They liked nothing better than sitting at a camp fire
blethering.

★

It was around this time that Smedley asked my family to pick the berry leaves from the fields he was pulling out. He had a kiln to dry the leaves out. Once dried, they were used to make aspirin and maternity tea. We made a lot of money doing that. It had always been a struggle in the winter time, but we weren't so badly off now we could get a few gigs to see us through. My father continued hawking as well – as he always said, 'Travellers could sell sand to the Egyptians.'

Around this time, the Chief died. My parents were pretty cut up about it. 'Another auld traveller gone,' my mother said.

'Aye,' said my father, 'it's all the good yins that's going. Well, there's one thing, Belle, he will go to heaven, if ever there was such a place, because he slept with his Bible. Even if he couldn't read it, he kent it was the holy book.'

The Chief was buried with his Bible in Dunkeld. A few days later, Willy Kelbie came to stay with us. He used to just come back and forward as he liked. He was a great help to my father, and could he play the mouth organ! Oh my God, he was the best mouthy player we had ever heard. No one had taught him; he had just picked it up himself. Hamish Henderson recorded him and his music is now in academic archives. He was harmless – he would never hurt anybody. He was a cheery creature who loved music and he never married.

★

My husband, the kids and I moved to Dundee because my two boys, Ian and Hamish, got houses there. When berry time came round, my husband and I and the other two boys moved back to Blair to stay with my mother and father for the berry season. On 8 August, it was my son Ian's twenty-first birthday. My husband said he would go through to Dundee and give our son his present, and asked me to stay and go to the berries with my mother because we had no money. We went along to a farm in New Alyth to pick. We finished about four o'clock, and when I got home my husband Ian was waiting for me. 'Have you any fags?' he said. I hadn't any. So we decided to go down to the shop and get some, and buy fish suppers for tea. My mother looked after the two boys while we were out. We got the cigarettes and were making our way to the chip shop when one of my husband's pals waved us down in the car. I stopped and my husband Ian rolled down the window. His pal said he was going fishing and wondered if Ian wanted to join him and a few others. Ian said he was too tired and just wanted to go home, as he had been all day in Dundee, but of course his pal persuaded him to go, and he didn't come home that night. Ian was a great singer and played the guitar, and he was always asked to parties to entertain. I was fuming, because that meant I had to go to the berries on my own again.

So next morning, my mother and I went back to New Alyth again with the kids. At about two o'clock, I looked up my drill and saw two policeman walking down. My mother and I started to panic. We had been never in trouble with the law in all our lives. They approached us and asked me if I was Sheila MacGregor. I said, 'Yes, I am.'

'Well, come with us please. I presume you have a car?'

'Yes, I do.'

'Well, we will follow you home to Yeaman Street.' I begged and pleaded with them to tell me what it was all about, but they wouldn't say a word. When we arrived back at the house, Cathie and Jimmy were waiting for me and Cathie was crying her eyes out. The policeman came to my car before I could get out, because he didn't want Cathie just blurting it out.

'I am sorry to tell you Mrs MacGregor, but your husband's body was found this morning on the bank of the River Ericht by two children on their way to school. I am afraid you will have to come with us to identify him.'

Cathie said, 'We were over, Sheila, and it is him.' But the police wanted his next-of-kin to identify him. My mother and I went over to the mortuary in the police car. When we saw him, it took me ages to speak, but finally I said, 'Yes, that's him.' I won't say any more about this, but the whole family was in a terrible state.

I didn't stay long in Dundee. I came back to live with my mother and father in Rattray and I never went back to the berries that year, as you can imagine. We went to Forfar sale the next month and I sold my car to get money to keep us going. We did get a few gigs and that helped a lot, but my father and mother got a lot more than I did, because I had the bairns to look after. Sometimes Cathie would go along and that helped her out as well.

★

Willie and Bella turned up one day and asked us if we wanted to go for a run in the car and take sandwiches and a kettle to make tea. So we agreed. We went up to the Falls of Leny, near Callander, a beautiful place for the tourists, and when we got there, Wee Turdy was standing piping. I never knew his real name – as long as I'd know him, he had always been called Wee Turdy. He couldn't play the pipes very well, and he had a couple of slates missing. He never made a lot of money. He was so pleased to see us getting out of the car when we arrived. We boiled the kettle and had our tea and sandwiches, and shared them with Turdy. He said to Big Willie, 'Will you hold my pipes till I go up this bank for the lavvie?' So Willie took the pipes. While he was up on the bank, a bus came into the lay-by. Wee Turdy flew down the bank when he heard the bus engine, grabbed the pipes and started to play to the bus-load of nuns who had arrived. At one point, he turned round and we saw the bottom of his kilt at the back was up, stuck in his belt. We tried to tell him, but with all the laughing that was coming from us, no one could speak. If he had stood still it would have been ok, but he was birling round to the music. Well, I never saw nuns move so fast in all my life. They got back into the bus and it drove away. They never gave him a penny. My parents told him about his kilt being up at the back and he laughed his head off. 'Well, at least they've seen something they haven't seen before.' That slate wasn't missing in his head anyway. Turdy made our day. My father gave him a couple of pounds, and so did Big Willie, so we paid him for entertaining us.

★

The first part of this tune was written by my father, and was put to the words of the song 'Fine Standing Man', by my son Ian. The second part was written by Willie MacPhee.

The Belles of Loch Lochy

1st two parts by

3rd & other parts by

*

One afternoon, my mother looked out the window and saw a man coming down from the pub, staggering all over the pavement. Then he fell into the road. My mother shouted for my father. 'Alex, there's a man fell on the road – it's the man that lives at the bottom o the hill. He is going to be run ower wi a car.'

So my parents ran out, and tried to get him up off the road. He looked at them and said, 'Get your tinky hands off me.' They could not get him to understand that he was lying on the road. They shouted for me to go down to the bottom of the hill and get his wife. She came up with me very grudgingly, and I thought it was because she was angry with him for being drunk, but no, it was because we had tried to help him.

When she arrived, we stood back and he got to his feet, then pulled her down beside him. He looked at her and said, 'Not now, and not here, maybe later.'

'You fool,' she said, with her face pure red. 'Come on, they tinks have seen enough of us for one day. Awa in tae your hoose and pick the lice off each other, and no smit us. That's all you're good for.' No thanks for letting her know her man was in danger. We were used to that kind of talk from the non-traveller.

Well, my mother started on her. The woman was known as 'the bike o Rattray'. 'I don't think you ken who your man is,' my mother said. 'You have bairns tae every man in Blair . . .' She went on and on. Oh, my mother gave her a tongueful that day.

*

The scrap my father was gathering was getting a poor price, so he said to my son Ian, 'Would you come up the glen wi me and Willie this year, as I am no able to stand all day piping, and I cannae let Willie dae it all himself. I will be able to pipe some as well, and your ma (that's what the kids called my mother because she said the word 'Granny' made her feel too old) can sell the heather wi Bella.'

'Of course I will, Da,' said Ian. ('Da' is what the boys called my father.) My father didn't play the pipes so much that year as he was ill. My mother looked after him well, and Ian played the pipes all summer with Willie. My father played a bit now and then, when he could.

My mother, my father and Ian left the glen the day after Big Willie. They stopped on the way down to Blair to make some tea, but they had run out of Calor gas, which is what they cooked on in the trailer. My father said he would make the fire. Ian went off to go to the toilet. So my mother decided to go down the bank and fill up the kettle with water. She filled it up, but coming up the bank, she slipped, and the spout of the kettle went into her cheek, just missing her eye.

She had the mark of the kettle in her cheek and the blood was pouring from her. She started shouting and my father heard her and went to see what had happened. What a shock he got when he found her and saw all the blood. He took her back to the trailer, and when Ian came back they drove straight home. The mark took ages to fade, but it finally disappeared and you wouldn't know it had been there at all.

Soon after, my father became really ill again, and had to go back to hospital for more blood. He was getting weaker and weaker. Even when he felt better after coming out of hospital, he wasn't the same man. He had no strength at all and he wasn't able to go on stage and perform ever again. So Cathie and I would go to performances. Sometimes my mother also went and then my sister Rena would look after my father.

*

Cathie and I were once down in Bristol doing a few clubs and were staying with my cousin's mother-in-law. We performed in one club and the following night we were preparing for the next one when the phone rang. It was my mother telling us my father had died. I dropped the phone and Cathie lifted it. My mother spoke to her and told her the news. She told my mother we would be straight home. We apologised to our hostess for having to go, and she said she would get in touch with the person who ran the club to explain. She told us to take care going back all that way in the state we were in.

Well, we started our journey. Cathie couldn't drive in the dark, so I had to drive all the way from Bristol to Blairgowrie. It was the most nightmarish journey I have ever had. We didn't stop once, not even at the services for a cup of tea, because we were so desperate to get home to my mother and the family. My dip-light failed, so I had to come up the road on full beam. There were a lot of angry motorists on the road that night, I can tell you.

We arrived home in the early hours of the morning, picked up my mother and went into Ninewells Hospital. We went straight to my father's room, but the bed was stripped and he wasn't there. We asked the nurse where he was as we wanted to see him. 'I am sorry,' she said, 'he is in the mortuary and you can't see him. Are you taking him home?'

'Yes,' we said, 'of course, as soon as we can.'

They didn't have to give him a post mortem as they knew he had died from pernicious anaemia. We took him home the next day, and that morning before he came home the minister from Rattray church came to see my mother. 'You know, Mrs Stewart, I cannot conduct the service at your father's funeral. He wasn't one of our parishioners.'

'But we have been in Blair all our days,' she protested. 'We were never allowed into your church, because we were travellers.'

'That may be so, but I don't think our congregation would be happy.' Then he left. We were devastated. One of the ministers in Blair must have got hold of the news somehow, because we got a phone call from a minister in Dundee called Hector McMillan. He said he would be proud to take the service for my father's funeral. We were delighted, I can tell you. Later on that night, my father's body came home. He was taken into the bedroom after we had cleared it out. He was in his coffin, which they put on trestles. They took the lid off the coffin as we requested and he looked as if he was just sleeping. All the family gathered round and took it in turn to stay up for three nights. Travellers from all over Scotland came to sit up with us. There was storytelling, cups of tea and food for three days and night, just like at an Irish wake.

All the kids in the family gathered the next day to see him. We believe in letting children see the dead and we couldn't help laughing at my sister Rena's wee boy Michael. After he came out of the room, he looked at my mother and said, 'Ma, how is Da lying in his pipe box?'

My mother said, 'Because he wanted to, darlin.' That satisfied him and he kept running through the room to look at him. Some folk would think this is terrible for a child, but you must remember it was part of our tradition to do this.

After the three days were over, he was taken to Alyth to be buried. Big Willie played the pipes at the funeral. Many, many folk singers came, as well as travellers, and Hector McMillan gave a sermon as if he had known my father all his life. We had no church to take him to, but we held the service outside his own front door in the open air, which made us happy. It was very appropriate.

There was a great sadness in Big Willie that day. After everyone had left the grave, only the family remained. Willie came forward, looked down into the grave, and said, 'Cheerio, my pal, I will see you someday,' and he threw a red rose into the grave.

As we looked at Willie, we knew his heart was broken. How he managed to play the pipes that day I will never know.

1980–1997

Some months after my father had been laid to rest, Cathie and I sat down with my mother and asked her what she would like to do. 'Well,' she said, 'there are only three of us left, and I think we should carry on the Stewarts of Blair tradition and keep singing.'

That is what we wanted to hear. A month later, we got a booking in Bologna, and my son Ian came with us as the piper. There was a festival and we had to go up into the mountain villages and perform. It was a wonderful tour and my mother really enjoyed it.

One night, in the hotel, Cathie said she was going to wash her hair, and grabbed the towel to go into the bathroom. My mother spotted that Cathie had taken the big towel and left the wee one. 'Quick, Sheila,' she said, 'go and get the big towel fae Cathie, because I want to take a bath and need the big towel. Give her the wee one.'

Well, Cathie was holding her head over the bath using the shower in her hand. I burst in and shouted to her and she got such a fright that she threw the shower up in the air. It was sky-rocketing all over the bathroom, and we couldn't catch it. We were soaked. Finally we managed to stop it and when we came back into the bedroom, we couldn't tell our mother what had happened because we were laughing so much. So she started to laugh as well, although she didn't know why she was. Finally we told her, and guess who got the big towel to dry themselves off with? Well, you can guarantee it wasn't my mother. The next day, we went up into a village in the mountains and were given a champagne reception from the lord mayor.

We weren't long home from Bologna when we got a phone call, asking us to perform in Lake Como for another festival. We agreed to go, with my son Ian as the piper again. So once again, we flew out to Italy. We arrived by plane and then had to take a train to where the organisers were to pick us up. We got on the train without problems but we couldn't get off for all the people trying to get on. My mother was shouting, 'Ged dear, we're gaen to be mouded wi this cull hantle.' We were creasing ourselves laughing at my mother, and I am afraid we were of no help to her at all. Eventually, a man stood up and mumbled something in Italian to the people who were getting on to the train. They all stopped and made way for us to get off. We were amazed. The man was wearing a hat, and he took it off, bowed to us, and sat down again. What a relief it was for us to be rid of that train journey, 'I am not doing that again,' my mother said, so, later, when it was time for us to leave the festival to go home, a girl drove us to the airport.

During our stay in Lake Como, we were walking along the beach. The weather was so hot my mother said, 'Let's go for a walk into town and see some of the sights.' We went up a long street until we came to a square where there was a cathedral. The doors were open, so we went inside. It was unbelievably beautiful, so we wandered about all the statues there, and we came to a statue of Jesus lying on a slab of stone. As we were looking at it, a woman, her head covered in a black scarf, came up to us and started shouting in Cathie's face, screaming her lungs out in Italian. We couldn't understand what she was saying. The man who looked after the cathedral dragged her away and sent her out the back door.

'What was that all about?' Cathie asked the man. 'I thought she was going to hit me.'

'She might have done if I hadn't put her out,' he replied.

'What did we do?' my mother asked.

'Well,' said the man, 'none of you had anything on your head, and you had bare arms. Never mind her, it is her custom. We get tourists in all the time who don't comply with her rules. You just picked the wrong time – coming into the cathedral while she was here. I am terribly sorry about that.' We didn't go into another church or a cathedral for the rest of our visit.

We had the night off and the folk at the hotel said there was music up at the square, so after our dinner we went up to listen. There was a stage and pipers were playing their pipes, but not the kind of pipes we had. The bag of their pipes was made out of a pig's stomach, with no cloth bag over it.

My son Ian always took his pipes with him wherever he went – he didn't want to leave them in the hotel in case they were stolen. He had them with him that night, so when the four pipers came off the stage, one of them went over to Ian and asked if he had pipes in the box he was carrying.

'Yes,' my son said.

'Are you going to give us a tune?' the piper asked.

'If you like,' said Ian. So he went up on the stage and played some jigs. Well, the folk started to dance every single one of them. My God, but they enjoyed themselves that night. They asked us to come back the next night, but we said no. We were booked to go somewhere else.

Two days later, we were back at home, sitting in my mother's living room. She was in the bath when the phone rang. I answered it and a woman's voice said, 'Is this Belle Stewart's house?'

'Yes,' I said, 'it is.'

'Is Belle there?'

'Yes,' I said, 'but she is in the bath.' The woman asked if I could give her a message.

'Of course,' I said.

'Well, this is Jimmy Veesy's sister. Tell her Jimmy has just died, and on his death bed he made me promise that after he died I was to let Belle know and tell her he never got married. She was his one and only true love.' I thanked the woman and she hung up.

When my mother came out of the bath I told her. She was very sad, but not as much as I thought she would be. Perhaps after all the years that had elapsed with my father, it didn't hurt so much. Or maybe she mourned in her own way, not wanting me to see her do so.

★

Late Last Night

O, late last night, I was asked to a wedding,
The wedding of a fair maid, who proved to be unkind,
As she looked in the eyes, of her new intended lover,
Thoughts of her old love ran still through her mind.

Supper was over and the sermon was ended,
And every young man had to sing the bride a song,
Till it came to the turn of her old intended lover,
Thoughts of her old love ran still through her mind.

'O, how can you sit at another man's table,
How can you drink of another man's wine,
And how can you lie in the arms of another,
When oft times, dear, oft times, you have lain in mine?'

Sobbing and sighing, she ran to her bedroom,
Sobbing and sighing, she went to her bed,
And early next morning, her bridegroom awakened,
And turning around, he found his bride was dead.

'O, Annie, dear Annie, I knew you never loved me,
My love and your love would never agree,
For I kent fine, I ta'en ye fae a better,
O aye, a better than ever ye could be.

I will put on my suit of deep mourning,
Suit of deep mourning ain, twa and three,
Then I will put on my new wedding garments,
To remind me dear Annie that you married me.'

*

My mother had seen a woman in Italy with a rinse of blue hair and she fancied it for herself. So Cathie said she would dye it for her. I was down shopping the day Cathie came over with the dye. My mother said she wanted it done in the bedroom in case anyone came in and saw her.

So they went into the bedroom and Cathie put a towel round my mother's shoulders. Then she started to put the dye on. It had to stay on her hair for ten minutes to give it a bluish tinge. After the dye was on, the phone rang. Cathie ran to answer it. It was someone ringing to book us to do a few clubs in England, so Cathie was gone for half an hour. She had completely forgotten about my mother until she came off the phone. She ran back to the bedroom and saw that my mother's hair was deep, deep blue, so she hurried her into the bathroom to wash it off. Well, she rinsed and rinsed it, but to no avail – it stayed a deep blue colour. Cathie made a quick exit home, and when I came back I couldn't get into the house for the smell of bleach.

My mother tried vim on it, brushing it with a scouring pad, but nothing worked and her head was red raw with all the chemicals she was putting on it. I felt so sorry for her, but I had a secret giggle when I was on my own. My mother was shouting, 'Cathie need never come here again! She better stay away from me for the next six months!'

I went down to the chemist and explained it all to the woman, who told me not to dye it again for about a week. 'If you do, it will turn orange and make her feel ill.' Back then, dyes weren't as good as they are today. So my mother stayed indoors for about a week.

*

We had been invited to Keith Festival, and we went there a few weeks later. There was a man there named Tim, who took a fancy to our friend Lizzie. Lizzie's man was with her, and she told Tim this. But no, no, no, he wasn't paying any attention to what she said, so she went over to him and said, 'Belle Stewart is looking for a man.'

'Is she?' Tim asked. He went over to talk to my mother, who was civil to everybody. She always had a twinkle in her eye and she flirted with all the men, but the men who knew her realised it was just harmless fun. This man, though, took it the wrong way.

Well, when the night was over we all came out of the pub and there was the man waiting for my mother. He put his arm around her shoulders and tried to walk away with her. She turned to him, swung her handbag and hit him square between the eyes, shouting, 'You dirty low-down whoremaister! Run before I crucify you!' Lizzie nearly wet herself laughing at my mother. She told her it was she that had put him on to my mother. Well, the two of them started laughing, and Cathie and I joined in.

★

It is terrible how times change, but I suppose they must. My mother was sad because travellers aren't the same any more: they can't stay where God intended them to stay, in the open air, and as free as a bird, with no worries about where to pitch their tents. That way of life is gone forever. What she missed above all was not getting out and mixing with travellers at their campfires. So one day we decided we would take a tent and go camping again. I got a roof-rack for the car, packed up the tent, found our outside cacavie and away we went. We didn't know where to go, and we didn't care, so we headed up to the west coast. It was a lovely day. We pulled into an old camping ground where travellers used to camp. We put our tent up, made a fire, and put the cacavie on for our tea. My mother was determined to make the same tea as the travellers of our family had done long ago.

She put into the kettle a quarter of loose-leaf tea, one pound of sugar and a pint of milk, and left everything stewing at the side of the fire. My mother said it would attract travellers to come to this place as they would be able to smell the tea 'all the way fae Oban'. I burst out laughing. We were sitting at the fire with the reek in our faces, eyes stinging, but we stuck it out and let it happen and never moved. Yes, my mother had gone back in time, and she felt great about the whole thing.

Just about three o'clock, a strange thing happened. Some travellers came round the corner pushing a pram with tent sticks tied to it. It was a man and his wife and one wee lassie. My mother jumped up to greet them – she was so excited that other travellers had come. They said they were moving on to some place down country to where their son lived, and were going into a house. 'Honest tae God sister,' the man said, 'there is nae place for us travellers tae bide nooadays, I doot wir travelling life is over.' You could hear the tremble in his voice. My mother persuaded them to stay for a couple of nights to keep us company, and they agreed.

'Div ye ken this, sister?' he asked my mother. 'I smelt the tea five mile up the road!' and he gave a wee laugh.

'You can use our fire tae cook on, if you like,' I said.

'Oh dear,' said the woman. 'Thanks, but it will be easy cooked. We've got bread and margarine.'

'Well at the very least I can gie ye butter,' my mother said and laughed. 'I will make a big slorach the night; I have a pot that wid feed seven navvies.' We all laughed our heads off.

My mother went to the nearest shop with the car and bought more tatties and sausages for a big sausage slorach. We also got the wee lassie some sweeties and a bag of crisps. By the time we got back, the man had his tent up, and there was a blazing fire going. The contentment on my mother's face was great to see. I thought to myself, we did the right thing bringing her up here.

We put the pot on after we had gone for water at a wee stream close by. The woman helped us to peel the tatties. 'God bliss my soul,' said the man. 'Aye, seven navvies and the half o Oban as well!' We really enjoyed our meal that night, placed on our laps.

We were never ones for tables, even at home, so we sat with the plate 'intae our gowles' – on our laps – as always. I still eat like this to this day.

The police turned up not long after we finished eating. 'Well, well, what's going on here, may I ask?'

'Well,' said the man, 'we're just havin something to eat.'

'You know fine that's not what I meant. Camping here is forbidden, you know.'

As quick as a flash I said, 'This gentleman said he could get our car to go, as it broke down, and we will be away as soon as it is fixed, officer.'

They were not bad police at all. 'Alright,' they said, 'we will overlook it this time, but we will be back in a few days to see that you are gone.'

The traveller man hated the police, and when they were going away, he said under his breath, 'Bing your badge into your jurival.'

The policeman turned around and asked, 'Did you say something?'

'Yes sir, I did. I burned my finger at the fire a wee while ago, and I was mumblin wi the pain.'

'Alright,' said the policeman. 'Two days, mind.'

We were so happy we had two more days to stay there.

Well, after the police went away his wife said, 'Willie you will get us banished.'

'I couldna help it, Mary, you ken how I am wi the man wi the white buttons.' A lot of travellers, including my father, called the police 'the men wi the white buttons'. It wasn't a derogatory statement, but as you may have noticed, travellers have different expressions for nearly everything – to me that makes us special.

We sat round the fire that night, cracking away. After a time, my mother said to them, 'We are sittin here and we don't even ken each other's names.'

'Well,' said the man, 'my name is Willie Johnston, and my wife is Mary Stewart.'

'Oh, ged dear,' I said, 'Stewart is our name as well.'

'Maybe we are related,' said the woman.

Well, she and my mother went through relations, all night, and the man must have known who they were talking about, because he puffed on his pipe contentedly. Mary stopped for a minute. 'Willie, gie me a wee plug ootae yer pipe.'

'I cannae, woman, I am still smoking it.'

'Aye, I ken, but you have plug in your other yin, have you no?'

'Aye, I dae.' So he raked the tobacco out with his pocket knife, and it came out in a hard lump. She sat quite content, chewing away at it. It turned out the woman was the granddaughter of my father's cousin. We talked till one o'clock, then we all went to bed.

We woke up the next morning at about nine o'clock, but there was no sign of Mary and Willie getting up. You see, travellers love their bed and never get up early except if they have work to do. They eventually got up at twelve o'clock, bleary-eyed, hair standing on ends – the usual way a traveller gets out of a camp in the morning.

Willie said, 'I think I will go guddlin in that wee burn this morning,' so off he went.

'He wilnae catch onything, he's moich,' said his wife. 'He never guddled in his life. I think he is trying to impress you.'

When my mother heard that, she remembered about my granny Nancy and the pot of eggs in Ireland. So she put a pot on to boil, although it was a smaller pot than the one Nancy had used. Two hours later, Willie came back with his tail between his legs and his head hung low. 'The fish don't want to get caught the day,' he said.

'Never mind,' my mother told him, 'I will soon have breakfast ready.'

The pot was boiling and she put two dozen eggs into it and boiled them for ten minutes, until they were fine and hard. She laid out two dish-cloths, and put the eggs on top of them. Then she made a wee pile of salt next to the eggs and threw some over her shoulder. 'My superstition,' she said. 'Now dig in.' We ate two each with toast from the fire.

'Dae you ken,' asked Willie, 'how toast was invented?'

'No,' we said. 'Well, this travelling family was camped at this camping ground, and there was country hantle stayin beside them. There was one slice of bread the travellers had left for their breakfast, between three o them. They aa made a grab for it and it fell oot o their hands. The traveller man grabbed it oot o the fire and it was toasted. Now the country hantle saw this, and was amazed at the taste o it, and that's how toast cam aboot.'

'Well,' said Mary, 'If you believe that, you'll believe onything. Awa ye fool, you just made that up.'

'No I didn't,' he said, 'it's the God's truth.'

We said goodbye to Mary and Willie and went on our way up to Oban, but when we arrived at Ganavan Sands, there was a big notice saying, 'No camping allowed'. Well, what were we going to do now? We headed back to the other side of Oban, where there was another camp there. 'We'll go and get groceries, and come back and put up wir tent,' said my mother. So we went to the shop. We would be about an hour, and when we got back, there was a bing of travellers and they were all drunk, roaring and shouting. So we reversed out of there quickly and decided to go home.

About three weeks later, my mother and I were in Perth, and who did we meet but Mary. She told us they now had a house in Fife, and that she often recalled the two days we had spent together. She told us Willie was working for a scrapyard, and was doing fine, but that it was murder getting him up in the morning to go to his work. She was doing a wee bit of hawking round the doors and her wee lassie was at school. She didn't look happy at all. I am afraid her life on the road was over, more's the pity.

★

This is a song that travellers always sang when they had a drink, and that was pretty often, I can tell you.

Johnny My Man

O, Johnny my man, do you no think o rising?
The day's far and spent, and the nicht's comin on,
Your siller's aa done and your stoups teamed afore ye,
So rise up my Johnny and come awa hame.'

'Noo, wha is't that I hear speakin sae kindly?
'Tis surely the voice o my ain wifey Jean.
Come in noo my deary and sit doon beside me,
'Tis time enough yet to be gaun awa hame.'

'O, Johnny ma man, when we first fell a-courting,
There was nothing but love then, tae trouble oor minds,
And we spent aa wir time 'mang the sweet-scented roses,
And we ne'er thought it lang tae be gaen awa hame.'

'I remember richt weel, Jean, the time that ye speak o,
And weel I remember that sweet flowery glen,
But they days are passed, and will never return, love,
So sit doon beside me and no think o gaen hame.'

'O, Johnny my man, oor wee bairnies are greetin,
There's nae meal in the barrel tae fill their wee wimes,
While you gang oot drinkin, you leave me lamentin,
So rise up my Johnny and come awa hame.'

So Johnny he rose and he banged the door open,
Saying cursed be the tavern that e'er let me in,
And cursed be the whisky that makes me stay thirsty,
So rise up my Jean, and we'll had awa hame.

Contented and crouse he sits by his ain fireside,
And Jeannie a happier wife there is nane,
Nae mare to the alehoose at nicht does he wander,
But contented wi Jean and his bairnies at hame.

★

My mother, Cathie and I were asked to go to a concert in Dundee. When we came out of the performance, there was a blizzard blowing, so we hurried into the car and made our way home. My mother said we would be better going by Alyth to avoid blocked roads, so we drove on the road to Alyth and half-roads to Blair, until we got stuck in a snow drift.

We were frozen, hungry and tired. Cathie and I were yapping away about our situation and my mother was saying, 'You should never listened to me, I'm nae driver, how would I ken what road to take?' Then she and Cathie started arguing, something they always did. I never argued with my mother, but Cathie wouldn't let her away with anything. Eventually they stopped and we sat there for about three hours, dozing off now and again. I woke up when I heard the noise of an engine coming, then I saw the lights of a snow plough coming towards us. It stopped beside us and the driver came up to the door of the car to tell us the road was open, but that we should be really careful. I went at a snail's pace all the way home to Yeaman Street. My mother lay in bed all the next day.

★

One day, in June – I don't remember the year – Hamish Henderson appeared at our door with an American. She was a collector from Boston. My mother was not so well that day, and couldn't be bothered to record for this woman. I remember it so clearly. She turned to her and said, 'If you want any recordings, you can get them from Hamish. He has been recording us for years.'

'Oh,' said the woman, 'I must have them from you personally, and Cathie and Sheila as well.'

She was talking down to us, not at us and she was showing too much authority, something my mother couldn't abide. My mother went to the kitchen and made tea. Maybe it was to calm down a bit, but it was a funny thing for her to do without saying a word. She came back with four mugs and set them down on the coffee table, then went for the teapot. When she came back the woman asked for a cup and saucer instead of a mug. She said she wasn't used to drinking out of a mug. Then she added, 'If you have any.' My mother was too quiet for my liking. Hamish was shamed to death, the way she was carrying on. My mother came back with a cup and saucer, put it down, and went to pick up the teapot.

'I'll pour the tea, Mum,' I said. I didn't trust my mother with the boiling tea, not at that moment, but as my mother said later, no one comes to her house without getting a cup of tea.

After we had our tea, I cleared the coffee table and then came back into the living room. My mother got up quietly, opened the inside door, then the outside door. She came back, grabbed the woman by the arm, dragged her to the front door, threw her out and banged the door in her face, then rubbed her hands together, turned to Hamish and said, 'Any more tea, Hamish?'

Hamish said he was so sorry, and that he didn't know the woman from Adam. 'I am sorry, Belle, but she is my lift home, so I have to go with her, but she will get a piece of my mind on the way home, and you can guarantee she will get no recordings from me of this family. This I promise.'

We were used to collectors coming to our house. Some were snotty and full of themselves, and some were great. But in all the time all these collectors came, we never got one penny for singing our hearts out, not even from Hamish. Lots of them thought we were only travelling people, and that they could do what they liked with us for nothing.

My granny would have said, 'You cannae talk back to the country hantle because they are educated and we are not.' As time went on, though, we soon learned that education is not everything. We have knowledge, something that half of them haven't got. We also have common sense. That was what our dear friend Hamish Henderson used to say, God rest his soul.

There is one thing I would like to clarify about my mother. People said she didn't speak as broad Scots as Cathie and I. In fact, she did, but when she spoke to the non-traveller, she slipped into a country hantle way of speaking. I once asked her why she did that, and she said, 'If I was to speak in my ain tongue they would never understand me.'

'But of course they would, Ma.'

'Sheila you have to respect them, and speak with a telephone voice. I have heard you do it on the phone.' You know, she was right. So even yet when I answer the phone, I smile and think of that.

Andrew and Sheila Douglas arrived the next day. They were true friends to my family and would come just to visit us. That relaxed us, because, to tell you the truth, although we were too polite to ever say 'no', we were fed up of having microphones stuck in our faces.

Whenever they came to visit, Sheila always did what the old travellers used to do and brought something along – a cake, biscuits, and, when my dad was alive, pigs' trotters. He had to shave the hair off them first, with his razor. We would watch as he ate them. When my father was alive, my mother would always say, 'I'm no kissin you for a month, mind, Alex.' I always laughed at this, because never in my life had I ever seen my mother and father kiss.

★

This story came from John Stewart, my father's brother.

The Silver Sixpence

There was this man that knew the people of a certain glen in Scotland, and seemingly when he came to visit the folk, they were grumblin and complainin aboot no gettin any milk from the coos. So the man says, 'What's happened?'

'Well, we take the coos in from the field for milkin, put them in the milkin shed. Then we go in for wir tea, and by the time we come out to milk them they are dry. Not even a pint between the lot of them.'

'Have you never seen anyone prowlin aboot the place?' he asked.

'No,' said the man, 'I've never seen a soul. Anyway, how could they get awa wi the milk? We would see them carrying it awa.'

'Are you sure you never saw anybody at aa?'

'No, not a thing.'

'Well,' the man said, 'when you take the coos in tonight, I will hide in the barn and keep watch.'

So that night, they took the coos in and the man got the old muzzle loader gun and loaded it up wi a bent silver sixpence. He was lyin amang the straw when he heard this scurrying noise and he saw a big brown hare. It lopped along and came in through a hole in the door, and went round every coo, one efter the other, takin all their milk. The man was so amazed, he didn't have the power to shoot. Just as it was going oot the door, he came to his senses and fired a shot. The men came runnin in. 'What happened?' they asked.

'I shot the hare. It was the one stealing all the milk.'

When they went outside, they found it lying there, dead.

★

All my mother's life, she had fancied a gold tooth and eventually she had gone and got one. My father, God rest him, had paid a lot of money for it.

One morning, years later, I heard her screaming my name and

I went to the bedroom to see what had happened. 'Sheila,' she said, 'I have swallowed my false tooth.'

I said, 'You have had it for years, Mum, and swallowing it won't do you any harm.'

'That's not why I am upset,' said my mother. 'That mongrel o a dentist said he took my tooth oot and put a false one in. Look, I still have my tooth. He must have put a cap of gold on it, and said it was a tooth, and made your father pay over the odds for it.'

'Well,' I said to her, 'there's no much you can do now, because he died ten years ago.'

'I feel naked without my gold tooth.'

'But mother, you still have the tooth that was underneath.'

'Aye,' she said, 'but you cannae flirt the same without a gold tooth. The two of us burst out laughing and we laughed until our sides were sore.

★

The berry time had come again. One day my mother said to me, 'Sheila, what do you say we have a while at the berries the morn?'

I knew she wasn't able, but I said, 'Alright, we will go.'

In the morning we got ready, made up a flask of tea and sandwiches and went down to the field in Blair. I will never forget my mother's face when they gave us baskets and told us we had to select the berries off the bush.

'What do you mean, select them?' my mother asked.

'Well,' said the man, 'you don't put over-ripe berries in the basket and you don't put under-ripe berries in the basket. They have to be selected off the bush. Oh, and no drinking tea in the field and no coming down to the end for a smoke. And you don't use the field for the toilet.'

Well, the look on my mother's face was a picture; she was completely shocked, and I felt the same as she did.

'I have never heard such ridiculous rules in my life,' said my mother.

'Yes,' said the man, 'it has changed from the old days, and

rightly so. We can choose who picks for us today, and we prefer the foreign students. They do what they are told, abide by the rules and don't grumble.'

'Yes,' said my mother. 'It's well changed from the time I made "The Berry Fields o Blair". Are you coming Sheila? I am no stayin to appear at this circus.' So we went away that day and never attempted to pick berries again. Those days were over now and this saddened my mother so much – no more singing in the fields, no more chatting and having a cup of tea with friends at the end rig. But my mother, being my mother, didn't dwell on it. When we got home she said, 'We got the best oot o the berries anyway, enough for a lifetime o memories.'

That is why not many local people go to the berries now. The farmers say we won't pick berries, but we in Blair are not used to all the new regulations now. So let them stay with their foreign students. If they are better, good luck to them.

For the travellers, not only is berry time over, but also the Dundee fortnight, and the Glasgow and Fife fairs as well. The worst part of all for us travellers is no more ceilidhs round the outside fire and no more sharing gossip or stories, or keeping up our culture as we did in days gone by.

'I know we have to change with the times,' my mother said, 'but I am too old now for their way o livin.' When we got home that day she said, 'We will hae wir flask tea and sandwiches on wir couch, and pretend we are at the field.'

'How can we pretend that?' I asked, laughing.

'Easy enough,' said my mother, 'imagination is the greatest gift of all. All storytellers should know that.'

Here is a very ancient story that many new storytellers tell nowadays. I haven't told it for a long time. I got it from my mother of course, when I was young. My mother would never forgive me if I wrote about her life without putting this story in.

Aippley and Orangey

Once upon a time, there were two wee girls. They each had a
pet name. One of them, Mary, was called Aippley and the other,
Jeannie was called Orangey. Now Orangey's mother wasn't
Aippley's mother, and Aippley's father wasn't Orange's father.
They were stepmother and stepfather. Aippley was an awful
bonnie wee girl and the stepmother was jealous of her, but wee
Orangey got on affy well wi Aippley, and really did like her.

  Wee Aippley had everything to do in the hoose, like all the
cleanin, while wee Orangey was allowed to go oot and play. She
felt sorry for her wee stepsister, but there was nothing she could
do about it, because her mother wouldn't let her. On Aippley's
birthday, her father went to the jewellers and bought her a ring
for her finger. He was very, very, fond of her.

  Now, one day when her father went to work, her stepmother
shouted on her as she was in the back garden. 'Aippley, Aippley,
come here at once!' So Aippley came runnin through the back
door. 'I want you to go doon tae the dairy and fetch the milk,
and mind you dinna break my good milk jug, or I will murder
you.'

  'I winnae, Mother.' So she lifted the jug an went skippin
doon the street to the dairy and bought the milk, but comin oot
o the shop door, she tripped and fell. The jug flew oot o her
hand and broke into smithereens. Oh my God, she didnae ken
what tae dae, so she sat doon on the pavement and started tae
cry.

  A man came up to her and said, 'What's upset you, wee lassie?
Why are you crying?'

  'Oh,' she said, 'I needna go hame tae my mammy, cos I broke
her good jug and she said she would murder me if I broke it.'

  'Never mind,' he said, 'it cannae be as bad as that. Come on
intae the ironmongers, and I will buy you anither yin.'

  'Oh! But my mammy will ken it's no her jug,' she said.

  But he went in and bought her a new one, then went intae
the dairy and filled it up wi milk, and handed it tae her.

  Noo, Aippley is flying hame because she is late. She looks in the kitchen and her mammy's no there. So she leaves the jug on the kitchen table, and goes back oot tae play wi Orangey.

Then shoutin came fae the hoose. 'Aippley, Aippley, come here at once! Where is my jug? That's no it!'

'I am so sorry, Mammy,' Aippley said as she came intae the hoose, 'but I tripped and broke your jug, and a man bought me another yin.'

'I told you what I would dae if my jug got broken, didn't I? Orangey, go down to the shed, and bring me that big axe, and mind and shut the door again.'

Wee Orangey had to do what she was telt fae her mother, because she was feart o her as well. Up she came wi the big axe fae the shed and the mother trailed wee Aippley oot o the hoose, placed her head on a block o wood and cut it off. Next she stripped the bones o flesh and put the flesh in a basin. Then she told wee Orangey to go doon tae the bottom o the garden and bury the bones. Wee Orangey did as she said, and her mother told her not to tell the father. She had a big pot boiling on the fire, and she said to wee Orangey, after she put the flesh in the pot, 'This will make a fine pot o broth for your father's dinner the nicht.'

When the daddy came hame that night, he walked in the door and said, 'What a fine smell o broth in here tonight.'

'Aye,' said the mother, 'sit doon and I will give you a bowl.'

'Where is my wee Aippley the nicht?'

'Oh, she's oot playin wi wee Orangey. Sit doon and get your broth.' She lifted the bowl and the ladle from the table, and began to put the soup into the bowl. During this time the daddy was breakin up his bread, waitin for the soup.

She put it down in front o him and on his first spoonful, he looked doon and there was wee Aippley's finger on the spoon, with the wee ring he had bought her for her birthday. Well, the father went stone mad, and never spoke to anybody for aboot a week, but it was done noo and nothing could be done about it. So things settled down again, but wee Orangey missed her wee sister terrible.

A few days before Christmas, the mother came hame one

nicht and said to her man, 'Have you noticed a wee white doo-doo flying around the hoose?'

'Aye, I have,' said the father.

Well, on Christmas Eve it was snowing hard, and the dove was sitting on their roof, and got up and flew away. It went up the high street, and all the shops were open wide for last minute Christmas presents. The wee doo-doo flew right up the high street, and right in through the door of the jeweller's, and sat on the counter. It looked up at the jeweller and said, 'If you give me the best pocket-watch you have in the shop, I will sing you a wee sang.'

The jeweller was amazed at this wee doo speakin to him and he said, 'If you can sing me a sang, doo, I will give you anything you want in the shop.' So it sang tae him.

> My mammy killed me,
> My daddy ate me,
> My sister Jeannie picked my bones
> And put them between two marble stones
> And I growed into a bonnie wee doo-doo.

'Oh,' said the man, 'I have never heard the like o that in my life. Take anything you want oot o this shop.' So the wee doo took the best pocket-watch in the shop and flew oot the door wi it.

Now the wee doo flew further down the street, till it came to a toy shop. It flew in through the door and sat on the counter, and said tae the woman behind it, 'If you give me the best doll in the shop I will sing you a wee sang.'

'If you can sing me a wee sang, doo,' she said, 'you can have any thing you want in the shop.' So the doo started to sing.

> My mammy killed me,
> My daddy ate me,
> My sister Jeannie picked my bones,
> And put them between two marble stones,
> And I growed into a bonnie wee doo-doo.

'Upon my soul,' said the woman, 'I have never heard better than that in my life. Take whichever doll you want.' So the doo-doo took the biggest doll in the shop, and off it flew again, further up the high street, till it came to an ironmonger's shop. It flew in, sat on the counter and said to the man, 'If you give me the biggest axe you have in the shop, I will sing you a wee song.'

'My God,' said the man, 'if you can sing me a wee sang, doo, you can have anything you like in the shop. So it sang.

> My mammy killed me,
> My daddy ate me,
> My sister Jeannie picked my bones,
> And put them between two marble stones,
> And I growed into a bonnie wee doo-doo.

'Oh,' said the man, 'that was marvellous, take whatever axe ye want in the shop, and good luck wi it.'

So the dove took a big axe and flew away till it came back to the hoose and perched on the chimney. It shouted doon the chimney, 'Orangey, Orangey, are you there?'

'Listen,' said the father, 'that's wee Aippley's voice.' So Orangey went and looked up the chimney – it was the big auld-fashioned one.

'I'm here, Aippley!'

'Well, haud oot your hands. I have a Christmas present for you.' Wee Orangey held oot her hands and this big doll fell intae her airms. She swung the doll round and round, she was so happy wi it.

The voice came again. 'Is my daddy there?'

'Aye, I am here.'

'Haud oot your hands. I have a Christmas present for you as well.'

So he held oot his hands as well, and the doo-doo dropped the watch down, and he caught it.

'Is my mammy there?'

'Aye, she's here.'

The mammy couldn't wait to see what present she was to get. She went over to the chimney and held her hands oot. 'I'm here, Aippley.'

'Stick your heid up the chimney to get your present, Mammy.'

The stepmother put her hands oot and stuck her heid up the chimney wi a smile on her lips. Down came the axe and cut the heid clean aff her.

★

We moved from Yeaman Street, down to live in Blair in a flat above a florist shop, right at the Well Meadow. In Yeaman Street we had no view, but now my mother could sit at the window for hours and watch the people pass by. She said to me one day, 'Do you ken, Sheila, this flat would have been your father's pride and joy, because every time he passed the Well Meadow, he used to say, "I would love a flat here, because you can see everything that goes on." '

It was great living there on Braemar night. We didn't have to go down to the street among the crowds; we could lift up the window and see everything. Braemar night in Blair is an important event on the calendar. The busloads come down the glen, after the Highland Games. They stop in Blair, where a lot of music played and there are mass pipe bands. All the pipers that have attended the Braemar Games that day get together and play around the town. There are also groups playing on stages, and crowds and crowds of people walking about, enjoying the music. So you can imagine how exciting it was for my mother to see it all from our own window. She was ecstatic.

She was getting old now, so I decided to have an eightieth birthday party for her in the Glenericht Hotel, in Blairgowrie. All the family came, as well as all the folk singers that stayed nearby. Andrew Douglas made a film with his camera and people took many photos. She really enjoyed that night, seeing all her family and friends. She was given many gifts and that made her happy as well.

Her memory was fading now, but her sense of humour was still there. She couldn't walk very far and this annoyed her, but with her being a little dottled, it didn't bother her so much. She was becoming senile, but she still recognised everyone who came to see her. The flat we were living in was a wee bit of a problem for her because it had an outside stair going up to the flat, and then stairs going up to the bedrooms.

I often took her out in the car to places she used to go – up Glen Isla, and to Forter, Glenshee and where we had the berry fields at Essendy. It brought back both sad and happy memories for her. It was a hard time for the family to watch such a proud and stalwart woman get old and bent, and what hurt the most was seeing her not being able to walk. But despite that, she was as happy as the day was long. Nothing bothered her now as much as it used to, and I was pleased to see her more content.

Looking after her, however, was a twenty-four-hour job. The doctor came to visit one day and said, 'Sheila, it must be a strain for you. We can put her in respite for two weeks to give you a rest.' He explained that she could stay in a home for two weeks to give me a break, and then I could take her home again afterwards. I thought about it with my kids, and they said I needed a rest. So I phoned the doctor, and told him that for two weeks I would let her stay in a home.

So my son took her to a home up the hill from where we lived. As he left her, she said, 'They are going to moud me here.'

'Don't be silly,' my son said, 'it's only for two weeks.'

'Where is Sheila then?'

'She needs a wee rest fae ye, Ma.'

'Did I get a rest fae her when she was growing up? I never put her in a home.'

The doctor told me not to go and see her or it would make her worse.

Only two days later, I got a phone call from the home, saying that she had escaped. My sister-in-law found her coming down the hill with a carrier bag in her hand. She had fallen down, she had a black eye and had skinned both her knees. I went down in the car to fetch her and she threw her arms round my neck. 'Don't put me in there again darlin, they would have mouded me.'

Old travellers had a funny fear of hospitals, and I should have been aware that this would happen, but I was so tired I hadn't thought about it properly. The only thing my mother couldn't accept was her non-independence. She regarded hospital as a prison, instead of realising that she was being well cared for by skilled nurses.

So she came home and, I have to say, I was happy to have her back again. From then on, a lady would come in once a week to sit with my mother while I went shopping. She was a godsend. My mother loved her and now didn't mind in the least when I went out. The woman also had a dog, Bossy, who my mother was always delighted to see coming into the flat.

She wasn't too senile yet, but I could see it happening slowly. For example, her cousin came in to see her one day. My mother looked at him and said, 'Who are you?'

'God bless my soul, Belle, you ken who I am,' he said.

'Indeed I do not, you could be a murderer, for all I ken, or a robber.' She honestly didn't know her own cousin. She kept looking at me and below her breath she would mumble, 'When is the coull bingin avree?' I apologised to him for her not knowing him, but he completely understood. It had been a long time since she had last seen him and he had a new beard now. Even I hardly recognised him. So I brushed it all aside and said to myself, she isn't getting worse. I kidded myself on for a long time.

The next year, we went to Kirriemuir festival, which had moved from Kinross to Kirrie. It was only fourteen miles up the road, so I said I would take her. She was excited to be going to a festival again, and all the way there she was reminiscing about when she used to judge the singing at the festivals.

We got to Kirrie and went in to the wee tearoom in the square where we had our tea. When we came out, she said, 'Sheila, I want to go home now.'

I said to her, 'But we haven't seen the festival yet.'

'I'm bad aboot a festival. I have seen more festivals than anybody. I want hame.' So I got her in the car and took her home.

When we got back, she said to me, 'How did we have to go to Kirrie for a cup of tea? We could have had it in wir ain hoose.'

I didn't say anything, because she would not have remembered anyway. I finally admitted to myself that her memory was getting worse and that we had to take every day as it came.

One day she looked at me and said, 'Will you sing me "The Whinny Knowes"?' That was her brother Donald's song. I was so pleased she had asked me to sing again after so long. I began to sing.

The Whinny Knowes

O, the lass that I lo'ed best o all was handsome, young and fair,
Wi her I spent some merry nights along the banks o Air,
Wi her I spent some merry nights, whar yon wee burnie rows,
Where the echo mocks the corncrake amang the whinny knowes.

We loved each other dearly, and disputes we seldom had,
As constant as the pendulum, her heart beat always glad,
We sought for joy and found it, whar yon wee burnie rows,
Where the echo mocks the corncrake, amang the whinny knowes.

O, ye maidens fair and pleasure dames drive tae the banks o Doon
You'll dearly pay for every cent, tae the barbers for perfume,
But rural joy is free tae all where the scented clover grows,
Where the echo mocks the corncrake amang the whinny knowes.

O, the corncrake is noo awa, the burnies tae the brim,
The whinny knowes are clad wi snaw that haps the highest whin.
When gloomy winter gangs awa and summer clears the sky,
O, we'll welcome back the corncrake, that bird o rural joy.

I looked over at my mother sitting on her chair. She was sound asleep, with two tears rolling down her face. I put a pillow under her head and left her.

★

Here is one of my mother's favourite stories, told in her own words.

The Headless Man

Noo, I would like to tell you this story that really did happen to a family called Reid. I suppose if you went far enough back they would be related to me, because my granny's own name was Reid. That's my father's mother, ye see. Noo, there is a place not far from the Beech Hedges, a place where, long ago, travellers were allowed to camp on as long as they liked, and it is called the Island of Kinclaven. It is just doon at the bottom o the Hedges. You turn on the Stanley Road there, and you could camp there for months and months if you liked. So there would be about eight or nine families aa campin there, and it was just comin tae the end o June. I ken it was the summer-time anyway, and this is what happened.

They were aa camped there and there was this young lassie and, just like the lassies nowadays, she had started courting, and that's going back a long time, even before I was born, and that's no the day or yesterday. This lassie noo was just coming up for sixteen and her man would be seventeen. The lassie's name was McDonald, and the laddie's name was Reid, as far as I was telt. This lassie took not well to having her baby, and it was her first bairn.

Long ago, it was always the oldest woman in the camp that attended to a confinement. The lassie was in labour for two days. You can't hurry these things, ye ken. The old belief was 'Let God take his ain time.' None o your new-fangled drugs tae hurry on your labour. After the two days o labour, this auld woman saw that there was something no right and that she couldn't do anything to help the lassie.

She turned to the lassie's faither and said, 'I think you will have to get the doctor, because she's no makin much o it, she's that young, ye see.'

Noo, all these things happened at a queer time o the night. So the faither o the lassie turned to her man, the young laddie, and said, 'You will have to go to Blairgowrie and get a doctor.' It was aboot five and a half miles from where they were camped into Blairgowrie.

'I will manage by myself fine,' said the laddie. 'I'll no take long runnin that road'. So he set off running up the road, till he came to the middle of the Beech Hedge. Then he heard a footstep at the back o him, but in they days it was nothing for folk tae take a walk at night. There was no buses in these days, and folk hardly used bikes. So he thought it was some o the ploughmen from some farm, and he never took any notice. The footsteps were coming nearer and nearer, but he wouldn't look roond because he was in a hurry.

By the time he was nearly at the top of the hedges, on the road to Blairgowrie, he thought to himself, I am going to look roond. He turned and looked. There he saw a man, and he would be about six to seven feet tall. It wasn't real dark at the time – it was gloamin dark as we say in Scotland, and he could see this man had no head on his body at all. The laddie got very feart and kept runnin. Then he put it down to his imagination, with him being all upset and excited because of the baby. So he thought no more about it till he arrived in Blairgowrie.

The laddie came to the doctor's door and the doctor asked the laddie where he was bidin. The doctors in Blair at the time were so used to travelling folk being in the area, it didnae bother them, and a birth among the travellers was quite an occasion for a doctor. They liked to be at it as it was quite a surroundings. The laddie told the doctor where they were camped. 'I know it well,' said the doctor, 'but I am afraid I can't take you with me, as I only have a Sheltie pony. Awa ye go home now and tell whoever is with the lassie to do nothing until I arrive. Hurry as quick as you can.'

Noo the laddie flew away and hurried along the road as fast as his feet would carry him. As he approached the Beech Hedge he got a wee bit feart. He thought to himself, 'That wasn't a man I saw wi nae heid, I just thought I saw him, wi me runnin so much and it being a fine summer's evening. I wonder what the time is noo, it must be getting on tae near one o'clock.' He realised he was awfa thirsty. Not far down the hedge, he saw a horse trough.

'God bless my soul, I could dae wi a cool, cool drink o water.' So he sat doon and he drank his heart's content o the water oot the trough, and he felt quite refreshed. He looked back, but there was nae sign o the doctor comin yet. He was feeling awfa tired by this time, and he thought to himself, 'There is no use hurrying noo, because I only have about a mile to go. I'll just walk.'

So he walked on and on until he heard these feet behind him again. He promised himself he wouldn't look back this time.

When he come to the bottom of the Hedges, where the clearing was, he looked round. And there, as clear as daylight, he saw that man again, but the moment he arrived at the last bit before the end of the hedge, the man disappeared and was never seen again. The laddie took to his heels and ran, and when he got back to the camp, he collapsed. He was so tired, he fell asleep before the doctor arrived.

The doctor hadn't a lot to do and a baby boy was born. The baby was about six pounds – a big baby for her being a slip of a girl, the doctor said. When the doctor had finished with the lassie, he asked to see the laddie. Somebody shouted, 'He is sleeping.'

'Ah,' the doctor said, 'I have to see him.'

So they got the laddie up, and told him it was all over, and that he had a wee son. Then he went to speak to the doctor. The doctor put his hand in his pocket and pulled out two half crowns, and he gave them tae the laddie. 'I was going to give them to your wife for the bairn, but you did such a wonderful job I am giving them to you.' So he bid them a good morning, and away he went.

Noo, they got kind o tired livin at that camp. They had been there about three weeks or a month, and they thought it was about time they moved on again. The young couple were the first to get ready in the morning for the move. She put her wee bairn in her oxter, and what wee puckle things they had into a bundle. They headed to Blairgowrie, because it was near the berry time.

On the road to Blair, as they were comin up to the bottom of the hedge, the laddie told his wife aboot this man, and where he disappeared. She laughed at him and said he was daft, and that he had made it all up. At aboot the middle o the hedge, the lassie said, 'I could dae wi a drink o tea.'

'Aye, and so could I,' said the laddie. 'I'll tell you what, just go up to the water trough and get some water, and we will make a cup. It's just up there on the left-hand side o the hedge. I will go to the fairm for a drop o milk, and maybe I'll get a piece fae the fairmer's wife.'

Noo, the laddie is away doon tae the farm noo, and he's been gone for a good wee while. He was tellin aboot his wife havin the bairn, and he is comin back noo, and he is pickin up sticks on the way back for a fire. When he comes doon tae where his wife was, she says, 'Honestly Davie, I have searched the hedge up and doon and there is nae trough there.'

'My God Almighty,' he says, 'give me the kettle and I'll get the water.'

Well, he searched, and searched, but he couldn't find any water either. So he said tae his wife, 'You sit doon there, and I will go tae the fairm for a kettle o water. I winnae be lang.'

Down he went to the farm for a kettle o water, and he said to the faimer's wife, 'What happened tae the trough that was at the Beech Hedges?'

'What trough, laddie? There never was a trough at the Beech Hedges. Are you sure?'

'Oh aye,' said the laddie, 'I had a richt good drink o it.' Then he told her about the man he seen.

'Come wi me', she said, 'tae the auld cattleman's hoose. He has retired years ago. He is nearly ninety noo.'

The auld man welcomed them in, and the laddie told him about the trough.

'Well,' he said, 'my family has worked at this farm fir nigh on
two hundred years, and there has never been a horse trough at
the Beech Hedges,' the auld cattleman said.

Then the laddie told the auld cattleman the story of the
headless man.

'Awa wi you,' said the auld cattleman. 'You're havin us on.
What kind o man did you see?'

So the laddie described him to the auld man.

'Well, laddie, I'm no going to say I never heard aboot the
man, and I'm no going to say I did. Take it fae me, laddie, that
man means you no harm. None whatsoever. In fact,' he said, 'I
think that man was guiding you to safety. But as for the water
trough, I think you must have made that up.'

★

The doctor came one day to pay my mother a visit, and he asked
her how she was getting on. 'Oh, me, Doctor, I am fine, but
you're no looking awfa well yourself. Are you feelin alright? You
are afwa peely-wally-looking, if I may say so.'

'I am fine, Mrs Stewart, it's you I have come to see.'

'Oh, well, you shouldn't have wasted your time, and I'm no
going back in thon home ever again. The last time you came to
see me, that's where I ended up, but no this time. Tell him,
Sheila.'

I was so embarrassed about the way she talked to the doctor
and I apologised for her. 'No need to do that, Sheila,' he said. 'It's
a poor world when we can't speak what we think, and that is just
what she is doing. I have known her long enough now to know
her wee quirky ways. If you need me, call me. Goodbye, Mrs
Stewart.'

'Aye, and the same to you as well, Doctor.' I don't think she
had caught what he said to her. He went away shaking his head
and smiling.

A story, just to let you know how bad her memory was at this
point: I had just fed her. She was a great eater – no problems
there. Just after I took the plate away, she turned to me and said,

'What are we havin for tea the night, Sheila?'

I looked at her and said, 'Are you still hungry, Ma?'

'Well a drop tea widnae go amiss, and nae bare-fitted tea, mind.' My mother couldn't take just a cup of tea on its own – she called it 'bare-fitted tea' if she didn't have a biscuit with it. Travellers have funny sayings like this, or at least my family did. If you were 'backet', you were dirty. A 'biscuit fit' was a hard, smelly sock. A 'cuphole of an erse' was a bed or a chair with a broken spring. 'You're a-buttert' meant that the legs of your trousers were too long and a 'creeshy weaver' was a fat person. These were all expressions we had made up in our family. I think my uncle Donald had the best sayings of all.

★

My mother was getting very bad on her feet by now, but it never affected her tongue, thank God. I went to the shop one day and she said to me, 'See if you can get any stottin bits.'

I laughed out loud, I couldn't help it. 'Mother,' I said, 'you cannae get stottin bits nooadays.'

'Your father got them all the time. Wait till he comes back – he will get them.'

I just looked at her and said, 'Alright, Ma.'

By the time I came back from the shop, she'd forgotten.

My sister Cathie had a party at her house for my mother's eighty-fifth birthday. It was a great warm summer's day, and we held it in the back garden. All the usual folk were there – Hamish Henderson of course, Margaret Bennett, a lot of folk singers and family too.

Someone asked my mother to sing and I listened with intent, but she would not sing. 'My singing days are over,' she said. 'I will leave it to the young ones now. Cathie, give us a song.' Cathie sang 'The Happy Auld Days is Awa'. It was Jock Whyte's song.

A couple of hours later, my mother asked me if I could take her home because she was getting tired. When we arrived back, I asked her if she wanted a shower. We had no bath, only a small cupboard shower that you couldn't turn in. She stared at me sternly, 'Indeed, by God, no.' she said. 'Do you mind the last time I went into that thick-lipped shower? You ended up coming in wi me wi all your claes on. I will wait till morning, I want my bed now.'

'Ma,' I said, 'it's only seven o'clock.'

'I'm no heedin, I want my bed,' she said.

So I put her to bed.

Things went on like this for another year. The stairs were getting me down. She now walked with a Zimmer frame and going to bed at night was torture, trying to get her upstairs. I had to push her upstairs by her hips while she hung on to the railing. It took us a good twenty minutes to get her into her bed.

I went to the council and asked them for a house on the ground floor. A woman came to see me and said I was first on the list, because my needs were great. They were building new houses in Rattray and I got the first one – an end house with a big patch of ground round the back and a wee picket fence at the front.

When I told my mother we were moving to Rattray, she thought I was sending her to a home again and I couldn't get her in the car. I had to phone my son Ian to come and help me with her. The occupational therapist gave me an electric chairlift to take her upstairs to her bed. It was wonderful. We were in heaven.

★

My mother and I settled down into our new house in Rattray. She had her special chair so that she could look out the window. By this time, she could hardly walk at all. Occasionally, my son Ian would take her for a few days to give me a wee rest. She would go with him anywhere, as she would with all my children.

Every day she would mumble to herself and I would ask her what she was saying. 'None of your business, my lady,' she would reply. One night, we were in bed. My mother had to have her bed in my room, because she would not sleep in a room of her own. I left the lobby light on as well. At three o'clock in the morning I heard her mumbling. Then she said, 'Cheerio then.'

I got out of bed and went over to her. 'Who were you speaking to, Ma?'

'Oh, Sheila,' she said. 'You just missed him – he came to see me – your brother Andy. I thought you were sleeping so I didn't wake you, but I am sure he will be back again.'

Well, that night I didn't sleep a wink, because my brother Andy had died a few years before. I thought about it all night and came to the conclusion that it was good, because she thought her bairns were still alive. In fact, apart from Cathie and I, the others had all died. Rena had been the first to go. Then, in the late 1980s, my brother Andy. A few years later, my brother John died, then Andy's wife Nanny and then John's wife. All these deaths happened within a few years and it had been very traumatic for my mother. When she used to ask for them, I would say they died and every time she would get a shock. So now I decided to go along with it and when she used to say, 'John hasn't been here for a while,' I would say, 'You know fine Ma he's awfa busy,' and that kept her happy.

'I suppose he will come when he is ready,' she would say.

It was a beautiful summer's day, and my daughter Heather came down to visit. She said to me, 'It's a great day, Mum, let's take Ma outside to get a wee bit o the sun. I think she would like that.'

So we got her ready and took her outside, put a jacket on her and wrapped her shawl around her legs and we joined her outside. I made a cup of tea. 'Brrrrr,' she said. 'It's gie cauld the day, isn't it? I think we would be better inside takin our tea.' She lasted about ten minutes. It took five to take her out, and another five to take her back in again. After we were back inside, she had the cheek to say she was tired with being outside so long. I couldn't help but laugh at her.

I was always frightened she would get out of bed and fall down the stairs, so I had bought her a bell to ring if she needed me. It was the worse thing I could have done. Every two minutes she was ringing it. 'I like the sound o that wee bell,' she said.

So I told her only to ring it if she needed me. 'But I need you aa the time, Sheila.'

'Yes, I know, Mother, but I have other things tae do.'

One day, I slipped the bell into my pocket. She never noticed, and soon forgot about it.

Once, I sat down beside her and sang 'The Berry Fields o Blair'. I asked her whether she recognised the song. She looked at me and said, 'Well, I've heard it before, someplace, but where I cannae mind.' I just left it at that.

★

On her ninetieth birthday, I organised a big party at Keathbank Mill, which had been turned into a function hall. It was ideal for the amount of guests coming. There was also a film crew who turned up for the event, and Blairgowrie Council sent a representative with a certificate to present her for her achievements to the town.

I have wonderful photos taken there that day. The food that the family had made would have fed two armies. There were strawberries as big as your fist, and of course plenty of raspberries too. Many, many folk singers came from all over the world and they all sang to her. First in was Hamish Henderson. My mother was mesmerised, and wondered why all her old friends were there. I had to keep reminding her she was there for her ninetieth birthday. She recognised some faces, but not others. Big Willie and Bella were there. My mother recognised them, and spoke Cant to them all the time they were there. No matter how senile she became, she never forgot her Cant.

She got tired early, so I had to take her home and put her to bed. On the way back, she stubbed her big toe and it bled a wee bit. She was diabetic but she wasn't on any pills or injections because her diabetes was associated with age and it wouldn't get any worse. Now, I didn't know at the time it was bad for her to hurt her toe, and especially for it to bleed. We bandaged it up and she went to bed.

The next day I asked her if she enjoyed the party. 'What party? Wasn't at a party for years!' she said.

★

One day, she wanted to hear pipes played. My sons weren't there to play for her, so I put on an old tape of my father playing. 'What's that?' she said.

'It's my father, your man, playing the pipes.'

'God forgive you, Sheila, I was never married, especially to a piper.'

That memory lapse didn't last long though, because next day she was telling me something that she and my father had done together.

My mother gave up singing a few years before she died. I used to ask her to sing to me, but she never did. She could no longer hold a tune and she had forgotten most of the lyrics. She wouldn't let me play any music in the house, either. She was quite content sitting in a quiet living room. The songs might not have been in her mind anymore, but she had them stored in her heart, and she knew it.

She lived for another two years after her ninetieth birthday party, and during that time her big toe continued to get worse. I dressed it twice a day, and the nurse came in twice a week to dress it properly, but it wouldn't heal. She didn't have to stay in bed though. The stair-lift chair meant she could come downstairs to sit in the living room. I came in one day and she was sitting on her chair, her arm was hanging down over the side, moving as if she was stroking something that wasn't there.

'What are you doing, Mother?' I asked.

'I'm clappin the dog, silly lassie.' I said nothing. I heard her telling the dog it was a good boy. She had had dogs all her life and if her imagination told her a dog was there, fair enough.

So there and then, I decided to get her a puppy. I scoured the papers for just the right dog for her. She didn't like big dogs – the last dog she had had was a miniature Yorkshire terrier, although I always thought it was too small.

The nurse came the next day and after she saw my mother she came down the stairs and said, 'I must call the doctor, Sheila, her toe is getting worse.' The doctor came a couple of hours later. I took him upstairs to see her and he examined her toe. He asked her how she was feeling, and as usual she said she was fine. The doctor and I came downstairs and he told me he would have to administer medication, which could not be done at home. So he said he would send an ambulance the next day. 'No,' I said, 'I will take her to the hospital tomorrow morning in my car.' It was only the cottage hospital in Blairgowrie, and my son and I could manage that. The doctor said she would only need to be in for about a week. Luckily, she was quite happy going in, because she knew it wasn't a home and that we wouldn't leave her there.

While she was in hospital, I found a dog for her. It was a King Charles Spaniel. I had to meet the owners of the pups halfway to Stonehaven. When we met, the woman had four pups in a cardboard box and asked me to choose one. They were all jumping around in the box except one, who was sitting quietly in a corner. 'I will have this one, please,' I said, pointing to the puppy. I took it home and from the first night the pup lay in his basket he was no bother and didn't cry once.

We went to see her in hospital the next day. She looked so poorly lying in the bed – she couldn't sit up. They were giving her morphine. I said to the nurse, 'Morphine is for pain, but she isn't in pain.'

'Oh yes she is,' said the nurse.

A couple of days later, my daughter Heather and I went to visit her. We sat at each side of the bed, holding her hands. Heather must have known something I didn't know, because she bent down, kissed her on the cheek and said, 'I love you, Ma.'

'Aye,' she said, 'I always kent that, darlin.'

Then she turned to me and said, 'Sheila, I am moudin.'

'Not at all,' I said and I could feel the tears well up in my eyes. I had to leave the room at that point. I walked up and down the corridor until the nurse came to ask me if I was alright. I said I was, but of course I wasn't. Then I went back in the room and sat with my mother for a wee while, holding her hand. I kissed her and said goodnight. She waved to us as we left. I sat up all night in the living room crying. Next morning, my daughter Heather came and knocked on my door at about nine o'clock. When I opened it, she fell into my arms. 'She's away, Mum.'

She had died at eight o'clock that morning. My son Ian had been in to see her after we had left and he was the last in the family to see her alive. You can imagine how we all felt. It somehow seemed so sudden. The doctor said that the morphine let her slip away peacefully. She never saw her dog and I still have him. His name is Prince.

Tributes to Belle

It seemed right for this last section to be written by my mother's family and friends, and by the folk singers whom she loved dearly. They need to have a platform to let readers know what they thought of my mother. I am extremely grateful for their contributions to her biography.

*

My mother was very proud of my daughter Heather, who went to nursing college. She is now a staff nurse in Blair Cottage Hospital.

Heather Brown

I was asked to tell my story about my grandmother, Belle Stewart. I must stress that I did not, nor ever would have called her Granny. To me and all her grandchildren she was called Ma. As I look back on my life from an early age, I can always remember how much of an influence she had.

I didn't grow up in a tent or caravan, I grew up in a house and went to school with every other child in society. However, the morals, values and culture I was brought up with were given to me by my grandparents. Don't get me wrong, I have devoted parents, but the biggest influence was from my granny. What she said, you did.

My memories of her when I was young were of a very upright, strong, respectful person with a heart of gold. I always felt secure when she was around because when she was, I knew that no one in this world could ever hurt me. She taught me to be like herself and for that I am eternally grateful.

An example of this was when I was eight years old and I had been bullied at school because of my traveller roots. I went home crying, but I didn't go to my parents, I went to Ma and told her what the kids had been saying to me. I could see in her eyes the anger but she told me something that is still in my mind today and it held me in good stead for the rest of my life. 'Heather,' she said, 'never show what people say about you; it takes a better man to walk away. Never go down to their level; always be respectful, no matter how hard it is. Show respect and you will receive it back.' Although I was very young at the time, she explained it in a way that I would understand. That was the start of a relationship that went on for the rest of my life. I told her things that I wouldn't tell my parents, because she could always see two sides to everything and that always made me feel better about myself.

I grew up listening to her stories and the songs and loved every minute of it. Ceilidhs were a way of life in my granny's house. Listening to her sing with her sweet voice was love to my ears, because every song was a story.

I remember once, she and my grandfather put me in their car and drove to a big building. I hadn't a clue what was happening. She took me by the hand and we walked into a big hall. Well, I can tell you I was scared. There were a lot of other children there and she walked up to this young woman, talked for a few minutes, then looked down at me and told me she would be back for me afterwards. No way was I going to question her. The next thing I knew there was the sound of Scottish music and some of the girls started dancing. That was my introduction to Highland dancing. From that moment on I loved it. My granny knew that if she had asked if I wanted to go, I would have said no, and for that I am grateful. I used to go busking with my grandparents up to Loch Lochy beside Fort William and dance for my grandfather while he played the pipes. Little did I know then that my dancing would take me to a different country.

I must tell you a funny story about this. A friend of Ma's wanted to take her to Austria, along with me and my brother, who played the pipes. Well, after thirty-six hours' travelling to our destination, we were staying in a hotel. My granny wanted to take a shower because she knew she was on stage the following day. I was sitting in the room when she said, 'Right, Heather, come on so I can have my shower.' I couldn't understand what I had to do with it but, as I have said, I never questioned her.

We went into the bathroom and she locked the door and made me sit on a stool. She then took off her clothes but left on her knickers and went into the shower. I said to her, 'Ma, why am I sitting here with the door locked watching you take a shower with your knickers on?'

'Heather,' she said, 'we are in a foreign land. You never know what can happen to you.'

I sat shaking my head and held my hand over my mouth so she couldn't see me laughing.

She was a character. There were other times in my life when she would do or say things that would have me laughing, but I didn't let her see me. I remember times when she would sit me down and teach me the folk music she loved. I learned them, but I must stress that I wasn't forced. I loved listening, especially when my grandfather played with her while she sang.

As I grew up and had a family of my own, she was still there, giving me advice. It pained me when she grew too old and her illness affected her. I will never forget the last time I saw her alive. She was in hospital (which she hated) and was lying in the bed. I knew she was dying and so did she, but no words were said about this. I sat there with my mother and I took a hold of her hand. I leaned over and kissed her on the cheek and told her I loved her. 'Aye, baby,' she said, 'I always kent you did.' I couldn't see her through tears. This woman lying in the bed was my Ma and I couldn't stop her leaving me. The pain of that day will be with me for the rest of my life. She has been and always will be an inspiration to me and the morals and values of the travelling culture will always be with me throughout my life. I only hope that my grandchildren will love me even half as much as I loved her. Even that would be enough for me, because my love for my granny cannot be described. There's still an inner pain when I think of her. Still to this day I miss her and the lectures she used to give me, and there are times in my life, and probably always will be, when I could do with her guidance.

★

This poem was written by the husband of one of Heather's colleagues at the hospital.

Belle Stewart

Belle Stewart came from travelling folk and how she loved to sing.
Music really filled her soul as she made the rafters ring.
World-renowned and respected, a person of great fame,
Though the humble start she had in life did not prophesy such
    acclaim.
A natural gift had Belle that just came to the fore,
The kind of gift that anywhere could open any door.
We'll all miss Belle and there's no doubt that we have lost a
    friend,
But the Lord above has gained one and Belle's legend will not end.
So Belle has gone to her just reward, in heaven where all is fair,
The angels will be lined up in welcome, singing 'The Berry
    Fields o Blair'.

★

Sheila Douglas

Belle Stewart is well known all over Scotland and beyond as one of the finest traditional singers of the folk revival of the 1960s and '70s. She always made a point of showing she was part of a family, by seldom wishing to perform without her husband Alex and her daughters Sheila and Cathie. They were all good performers, but it has to be acknowledged that Belle was the matriarch of her family's tradition. She was the 'floo'er abune them aa'. Among the travellers she was known as Granny Belle and in her own family she was known as Ma. The wider public called her 'Queen Amang the Heather'.

The settled population's view of the travelling people is based on assumptions about material wealth and social rank. Belle in fact was born into a cultural aristocracy and she eventually married into another great travelling family of famous pipers, singers, dancers and storytellers. The travellers had to look for many different ways to make a living. They were agricultural workers and the farmers were only too eager to employ them. They were also pearl-fishers, fortune-tellers and horse-dealers.

One of the earliest songs Belle wrote was 'Whistling at the Ploo'. She was at the potato-gathering and looked across to the other field where she saw a ploughman ploughing with two white horses an event that never happened at that time because horse ploughs had died out by then. So she wrote a song about it.

I had first heard the Stewarts in Perth Folk Club in the early 1960s, where they made a lasting impression upon me. Among all the kaftans, jeans and sweaters were Belle and Alex and their daughters Sheila and Cathie, who appeared in flowery dresses. Belle had on a fur coat. The three striking-looking women sang unaccompanied, with passion and style.

But before that, Belle and Alex visited my house, all because of a song, 'Dalry', which I had heard someone sing at the club. I asked him where he got it from, and he told me it was Belle Stewart. Dalry was the name of my father's birthplace, and I was very interested in the song. He wrote to Belle about it, and she and Alex came to see me. We were firm friends from then on. Belle's great songs were 'The Bonnie Hoose of Airlie', 'Tifty's Annie', 'The Dowie Dens of Yarrow' and many more. Belle had no need to learn new songs, for her repertoire was a full one. It was she who taught me and many more about the quality of the congnach.

When she died, I was given the honour of making a speech at the graveside. There were huge crowds of people at her funeral. Family and friends came from all over the country to see Belle laid to rest. The service was conducted by her grandson, the Reverend Hamish MacGregor. We all felt it was the end of an era and that we had lost a mother figure in Belle.

★

Dave Goulder

It would be the autumn of 1963. The unlikely venue was a house off Clapham Common, where the country singer Bill Clifton took his new friend and fledgling songwriter to meet a singing family from Scotland.

It was a revelation. The regal lady, her two pretty daughters, the serious-looking man and his humorous interjections while defending himself with his pipes. And the singing!

Over the years I learned that when Belle made a friend it was for ever. She must have met thousands like me, but the greeting was always the same: a huge smile of recognition, my name ringing in the air, an enormous hug, then, 'How's the family?' (She would name them all.) Then, 'Do you remember that day in Clapham?'

Once we were all at Newcastleton Festival, and the Stewarts were performing at the British Legion where there was a 'no children' rule. A jobsworth was stationed at the entrance and as I tried to smuggle my infant daughter through in a basket he caught my arm saying, 'What's in there?'

He in turn was restrained by a much stronger arm, and a voice with an authority that must have taken him back to his service days proclaiming, 'Nothing that would concern you.' If he had been allowed to leave his post and join the audience he would have revisited his past yet again when Belle launched into her 'First World War' set. From the crop-headed arthritic to the rope-sandalled daffodil – all were unable to resist the infectious enthusiasm of the true entertainer.

Now I too have joined the ranks of ageing arthritics, and whenever two or three of us meet it's inevitable that we recall those marvellous years when we were learning our craft. The names, the places, the laughs, the songs and the almost overwhelming presence of the personalities who led us in our chosen dance. Without any sadness I am pleased to write these few words for that personality who meant most to me, Belle.

★

Ken Hall

Some years ago, Sara Grey, after moving to a particularly lovely location in Inverness-shire, invited friends from both sides of the Atlantic to spend the weekend in the area. During a break in the singing, somebody commented on the beautiful scenery. Belle Stewart, who was one of the guests, replied that she was tired of beautiful scenery, all it represented to her and to the travelling community was hard work, which had to be carried out in all weathers.

This was Belle Stewart's life for the great majority of her ninety-one years. While the travelling life obviously had its attractions, it was no easy option. Much of the work which had to be done, such as the berry-picking in Blairgowrie, could be physically demanding. In addition to the harshness of her life, Belle had to cope with more than her fair share of personal and family tragedy. She also had to cope with the unthinking prejudice towards travelling people which still exists today. As Ewan MacColl's 'Moving-on Song' says, travellers were rarely allowed to settle in any one place for long; they always had to be moving on.

Belle, however, took all that life could throw at her and came out on top. I first saw her at the National Music Festival at Sutton Bonington in 1988. Her daughter Sheila and grandsons Ian and Rob Roy also came down from Scotland with her. In addition to her fine singing I will always remember her very bawdy sense of humour. Belle was out to enjoy herself that weekend. Concerts would be interrupted for minutes on end because the audience would break out into bouts of laughter at one of Belle's stories or jokes. She was obviously the leader of the family at this time, not just because she was the senior member but also through the sheer strength of her personality. The other members were told what and when to play or sing and there was no argument!

There is an old religious saying, 'the family that prays together stays together'. However, with regard to the Stewarts, it might be more apposite to remark that 'the family that sings and tells stories together stays together'. The Stewarts are still a very close-knit family, as any visitor to Sheila's flat will testify. Immediate and wider family members come and go and the door is never closed. Though Belle has been gone some years now, you still get the feeling that she is in some way presiding over events. I don't think there can be any doubt that all members of the Stewart family know that Belle was a very special woman. Throughout the travelling community generally she was obviously held in great esteem, as those of us who witnessed the amazing turn-out at her funeral will testify.

★

Gil Harper

It was a blow to hear of Belle's death in 1997. The twists and turns of life meant that I had not seen her for a few years and I felt the loss very keenly. Her influence is etched into the memory of my youth.

It was 1963 when I first met Belle and Alex Stewart. The occasion was the Centre 42 project which, under the direction of Arnold Wesker, was designed to take the best of collective creative and artistic traditions to the workers who at that time had no easy access to them. Organised by A.L. Lloyd and Ewan MacColl, our numbers were boosted by real folk artists, then called 'field singers', as part of a plan to show us what it was really all about. And so, in the company of the likes of Belle and Alex, Francis McPeake and Joe Heaney, we sang our hearts out in pubs, works canteens and working-class theatres of the then great industrial towns and cities of the English Midlands. It was a romantic ideal which was also a school of hard knocks as we braved flying chips in works canteens, thrown by disgruntled workers who merely wanted to read their papers and fill in their pools coupons. We marvelled that Bobby Davenport at full blast was the only one who could sing a jukebox down. It's not generally known, but Belle wrote a song about her Centre 42 experience.

On a rest day in Nottingham, a Sunday, I think I saw Belle, Alex and Francis wandering aimlessly through the town which was a stranger to them. To help fill their day in a congenial way, I invited them home for tea. There a mutual hospitality was cemented which my family treasures in memory.

Belle's story, like her ballads, is an epic which has now been ably told by her daughter, Sheila. What is undeniable is that she had a 'presence'; you knew that she was there regardless of whether she spoke or not. Quite clearly she was the matriarch of those around her. When staying with the family I felt was treated like a son and, interestingly, even today when Sheila and I talk seriously about things, we will often address each other as 'brother' and 'sister'.

To Belle it was all about feeling. Hearing her formidable delivery of one of the great Scots ballads, especially in her own home with friends, was an awe-inspiring experience. The delivery was straight, the air often unimaginably beautiful, fitfully subordinated to the story. Not for Belle the florid and often baroque decorations of Irish tradition, although she had much rare Irish material gathered from her travels in that country, but rather a direct approach where a slide, a grace note, a tonal emphasis, would illuminate the import of what you were hearing. The ballad finished, a silence, prickly hair on the neck, emotion welling, a burst of applause, the sign of a great performer. Belle could press that button any time.

Traditional storytelling is a lost art to the urban population of these islands. But the Stewarts were masters of a skill which is now being passed on by Sheila. When Peggy Seeger tells the tale of Aippley and Orangey she is telling a Belle Stewart story. Tale-telling alone could fill an evening and Belle and Alex could match each other. They were a good double act. Likewise, the telling and solving of riddles delivered with alacrity left the observer agog.

But the story of Belle Stewart surpasses her greatness as a ballad singer for it is a story of a family. The partnership with Alex was of such import that the family became known as the Stewarts of Blair, firstly in Scotland, then across Britain and the world wherever traditional music has a following. Belle was even featured on *Desert Island Discs*. It is clear that Belle was the catalyst in the mystical mixture which contributed to their heady brew.

One pleasant evening in their home, Belle told me some of the Stewart story, much as Sheila now tells it, with Alex interjecting the occasional 'Aye, that's true'. A ceilidh at the Stewart home was something else. This was not the Jimmy Shand event associated with Scottish Television, nor was it the country/barn dance event projected by the folk club scene. Here was the real thing.

One morning I awoke to an unusually quiet house. At midday Belle suddenly declared she was having a ceilidh. She sent me to a very small pub in New Alyth, The Blackbird, I think, to pick up extra supplies. Unfortunately, I was waylaid there by a bunch of happy Irishmen who had been digging a tunnel through 'The Grampians' and were newly out of their decompression chambers. No was not an acceptable answer to their company. Some time later, I finally escaped their hospitality, still clutching my precious load, and glancing back as I left, I could swear that the only thing left on the pub shelf was half a bottle of Green Chartreuse. Needless to say, when I arrived back at six that evening, I was late and the proceedings had already started. A running tractor had been abandoned and music was coming through the door of their New Alyth house. Mysteriously, a full complement of guests had arrived. Included was old Charlotte Higgins, a good and sound singer, related to the Stewart family network through marriage.

Everyone had to do something, including the children. There were songs, stories, riddles and party tricks. Alex retired to another room, as is proper with the Highland pipes, to play jigs and reels with a facility I have not heard before or since. Amidst it all sat Belle, the kindly matriarch, regal in her features and posture. In the early hours Charlotte, experienced and respected in such matters, quietly and confidentially read the tea leaves for Belle, and there you go, all was right with the world. The proceedings continued.

There is much I could still write in praise of Belle and her remarkable family, but perhaps this is best left to that folk memory to which their contribution was so massive, and to her daughter Sheila. For myself, I cannot look at the words of a folk song without hearing her voice and feeling the notes at the back of my throat. For you, listen closely to the voice of Sheila and you will still hear Belle Stewart, née MacGregor. The tradition lives on; she was a Queen of Singers.

*

This obituary was written by Hamish Henderson and first appeared in the School of Scottish Studies publication, *Tocher* (no 54/55), in 1998.

Hamish Henderson

Belle Stewart, the matriarch of the 'brochan' Stewart tinker clan, who became known to the world in her middle age as the author of the song 'The Berry Fields o Blair', was born in a bow tent pitched on the bank of the River Tay near Dunkeld on 18 July 1906.

Belle's maiden name was MacGregor, and the Canadian anthropologist Frank Vallee remarked, on their first meeting, that he now knew why Scott in *Rob Roy* had put in Rob's mouth the proud declaration: 'My foot is on my native heath, and my name is MacGregor.' No MacGregor, he said, can ever have justified that boast in his or her person better than Belle. She was quite the most regal person he had ever seen. This thought was echoed by the Irish folklorist Seán O'Boyle after he had been introduced to her: 'She looks like an empress.'

However, it was Belle's husband Alex who actually bore the old royal name itself: his grandfather was Big Jimmy Stewart, who combined undoubted fame as a piper with expertise as a 'traveller' salesman. He was piper to Lord Dudley. 'He'd gae doon in the mornin, and play roond the big hoose, and he'd be back at nicht playin roond the dinner table. In between he'd be up and doon the glens sellin dishes.'

Alex was, therefore, the descendant of a formidable clan of 'travellers' (i.e. tinkers) which could trace its ancestry back to 'Auld Jimmy Stewart of Struan' who crossed from Perthshire into the north-east Highlands in the early nineteenth century, and periodically returned with his people to Glenshee and the other Perthshire glens.

Much of Belle's early married life was spent in Ireland, and at its best the music she created exemplified a marvellous creative blend of Irish and Scottish 'tinker-gypsy' creativity. As for the gypsy element, it cannot be gainsaid that many of the traveller Stewarts and MacGregors, including Belle's own daughter Sheila, bear a striking resemblance to pure-blooded Andalucian gypsies.

Be that as it may, Belle's clan is undoubtedly the custodian of an amazing treasure-house of Scottish and Irish folk music. The way of life which has engendered and preserved this astonishing cultural phenomenon is nowhere better recorded than in Belle's own song 'The Berry Fields o Blair'.

Dear Belle, thanks for aa thing and farewell.

★

Jimmy Hutchison

I was living in London in the early 1960s when I first started singing in folk clubs (before that I had just sung in pubs and in the house) and when speaking to other young singers there were two names that were always mentioned as singers I must hear: Jeannie Robertson from Aberdeen and Belle Stewart from Blairgowrie. When I came back to live in Scotland and helped run the St Andrews Folk Club, I got the chance to meet both of these great ladies.

I remember very clearly the first time I met Belle. A concert had been arranged on a Friday night in the Victoria Hall and the Stewarts o Blair were booked to appear along with Archie Fisher. When Belle swept in (I've a sneaking suspicion that Belle always made an entrance rather than just walked into a room), I was knocked out by this vision in Dress Stewart tartan; she was very tall and very beautiful and I think I maybe lost my heart a wee bit. I'm not the only young singer that had a secret fancy for Belle in those days.

The concert was a great success but it was the party afterwards (there was always a party afterwards in the Sixties) that I remember best. Belle was great fun and had plenty of stories about the traveller's life on the road, not all of them repeatable here, but it was her dedication to singing that impressed me most, not only her own singing, which was special of course, but also the fact that she was very keen that the young singers should learn the songs and keep them alive. She was most encouraging and helpful to me and I still sing two songs she gave me that night: 'The Bonnie Hoose o Airlie' (accompanied by Alex playing on the Goose) and 'Queen Amang the Heather'. The 'Bonnie Hoose o Airlie' was particularly memorable here was a woman singing a ballad about an event that had happened right in the area in which she lived. She sang with such conviction it sent shivers up your back. I know I will never forget that night and I'm sure that is how Belle will be remembered by all who met her. She had a great sense of fun and a wonderful repertoire of songs and stories, but mostly she had a great generosity with her material and an enthusiasm for passing on her songs to future generations.

★

Gus Langlands

Nearly ten years ago, Dave Goulder and I were sitting in the audience at a concert which was part of a festival in Penicuik, listening to the singing of Jock Duncan. 'Isn't it amazing how they keep on finding these guys with old songs to sing?' was Dave's thoughtful comment. Then after a couple of moments he added wryly, 'Of course, you have to realise that one day, when we become *really* old, it's liable to be you or me they "find", with our old songs to sing!' It's true. Time rushes forward, the scenes of life change, people come and go, but there are a few rare souls who were such iconic figures in our musical landscape that their place in both history and our memories is assured for all time. Who could ever dispute that Belle Stewart has her special place in that select band?

Many people, far more knowledgeable than I, have written extensively about Belle's singing and her songs, so I do not propose to add much here to that already comprehensive record. However, I will say that her performances were always a delight to me and having been entertained by Belle, I would return home with a lighter step. I have tried hard to remember *where* it was that I first met her (it could easily have been in the early 1960s at St Andrews Folk Club, when it used to meet in the Star Hotel), but the initial impact which she had upon me is as fresh and indelible now as it was all those years ago. In some ways it was like meeting a second mother. She was direct, open, warm and welcoming, maternal, friendly, generous, spiritual, statuesque and extremely couthy. She had all the dignity and justifiable pride which comes from being in close contact with one's family heritage, but absolutely none of the arrogance and pomposity which often characterises the attitudes of lesser mortals. Belle didn't need a trumpet to blow, quite simply because the illuminating force of her personality commanded one's willing attention, without any contrived effort on her part. That's how people should be.

In those far-off early days, there was always a great welcome at that row of cottages known as 'Well Bank' in New Alyth, where Belle's family lived. I remember on one occasion arriving with a group of friends in mid-afternoon and being hospitably encouraged inside by Belle, who greeted me with the observation, 'I've only just put the kettle on and now I know why.' Of course, the usual ceilidh was not long in following and I have a clear recollection of being asked to sing whilst standing at the left-hand side of the fire above which was the high mantelshelf filled with polished brasses and doing the best I could with 'The Rigs of Rye'. It was always hard to leave that address, but those special shared moments are now treasured memories which form part of an immutable experience from those early days of the Revival.

Those of us who were privileged to receive an invitation to Belle's ninetieth birthday party will, I'm sure, never forget that afternoon of celebration and gratitude for all the pleasure she had given us for so many years. It was an honour to be there. As usual, the hospitality was of the highest order and, though confined to her chair, Belle clearly enjoyed the whole proceedings. I wouldn't have missed it for anything. For me, the high point came when she was finally persuaded to sing and she launched into 'Ah Wonder Whit's a Dae wi Aa the Men'. The cheer she received at the end was as warm, sincere and deserved, I'm sure, as any she'd ever been given in all the preceding years.

Sadly we shall never see her like again, but it is the duty of us all who care about music, the songs, the fellowship and the tradition, to ensure that Belle's legacy and her charismatic humanity remain alive into the future, as befits her unique place in Scotland's cultural heritage.

★

Kate Lissauer

I met Belle Stewart at Whitby Folk Week in 1986. It was a rainy summer for her grandson Ian, and he tired of trying to busk at Loch Lochy in the bad weather, deciding instead, at the last minute, to take Belle to the festival. I was there as the fiddler for the Steptones, a duet of synchronised Appalachian cloggers, and it was my first trip overseas. I entered a venue one evening as Belle and Ian were on stage and was charmed at once. She was a tall, commanding woman, regal of presence, and completely engaging in her performance. I am sure that the initial interest I took in her grandson, who I later married, was sparked in part by the charisma carried by Belle.

I lived in Blairgowrie for several years, and my social life consisted mainly of rounds of visits to my numerous new relatives. Granny Belle, or Ma, lived in an old stone cottage on Yeaman Street in Auld Rattray, with her dog Tiny. A welcome to her home always involved several cups of sweet milky tea with biscuits, and very often a full meal. She was always concerned that her grandchildren should eat well, and would occasionally slip me a pack of sausages as a special treat, believing that I would appreciate them as a way of pleasing my new husband. This habit struck me as gallingly old-fashioned at first, but soon came to see that her way of showing support was completely different from what I was accustomed to in the world I had come from.

Ma maintained a sort of portable travellers' culture of ritual and superstition which must have helped her to keep alive and valid her sense of identity, as well as helping her to feel safe. It was important to know some rules if one were to visit and spend time in her company, and it was very easy to make a mistake or faux pas if one wasn't fully indoctrinated. Once I gave her a plant, as a gift, and later found to my embarrassment that it had to be kept in a room far from hers, because she feared that a plant in the bedroom would rob her of oxygen and prove damaging, even fatal. I needed to know what names to avoid in the morning, and some names which it was best never to say at all. There were certain simple hygiene rules, which had surely derived from the practical necessities of life on the road, and rules about what to do upon entering and leaving a house.

Belle was a woman who was simultaneously slighted by the world and queen of it. She had a wonderfully double-sided personality, most likely as a direct result of being what she liked to refer to as a 'member of a down-trodden race'. She was unfailingly charming to visitors and strangers, perpetuating her image as a grande dame of the musical traveller's world. She had been spoiled throughout her life, by her doting uncles at first, then by her husband and by her fans, and she often behaved like a prima donna. But she also suffered many anxieties, hated being left alone, and was caused by her fears to be infuriatingly demanding. She could be hilariously petulant and critical when only family were listening. And she was a drama queen of the first order. On one occasion when she was staying overnight with us, and I was heavily pregnant, she fell down and called for me to help her, with all the anguish of one who is suffering terribly and probably mortally injured. I tried to lift her, but she was dead weight. 'I'll have to go and get Ian,' I said and turned away. The fear of Ian seeing through her must have motivated a speedy recovery, for a moment later, when I turned back, she had leapt to her feet and showed no sign of the slightest distress.

Ultimately, Ma proved to be one of the best allies I found in my in-laws' family, and this as a direct result of being part of a culture which I viewed at first as being bizarrely anachronistic. She held to values and practices which had been discarded as the younger generations of travellers were indoctrinated into mainstream society. As a result, she frequently gave me advice that I would not have encountered elsewhere, to do with bearing and caring for children, holding my own with my partner, and so on. (For example, if you want to increase the flow of milk for your infant, soak oats in water overnight and in the morning drink the resulting fluid.)

The broader picture, and the one I particularly hold dear, is of a talented and creative woman who transformed the experiences of her life through song, story and humour, and who made the most of her circumstances in true traveller fashion, turning hardship into romance and persuading us all to share it.

★

My mother was really proud of my son Hamish becoming a minister. She remembered the time when we couldn't get one from Blairgowrie to bury my father, but we have a minister of our own now, and there will never be a problem again for us. He is the Reverend Hamish MacGregor and this is what he wrote about her.

Hamish MacGregor

It's not too difficult a task to put together a few words to describe what Belle Stewart meant to myself as a member of her family. What I will find difficult is to know what to leave out. As her grandson, who has had the pleasure to live close to his 'Ma', there was seldom a time when she wasn't around. It didn't matter where we lived, whether it be this side o the border or the other side, Ma and Da were never too far away.

From my early years as a boy, visiting them always caused a leap of excitement in my heart and though these few words are dedicated to my granny (though I never ever called her that), Da was equally special to me. Between them both, they gave a meaning to my life that could never have been duplicated by any other living souls on the planet. In fact, to say I loved them sounds like an understatement to me. Personally speaking they were simply two of the most influential people I have ever known and cared about. Indeed, to think of my life back then as a boy growing up was truly to think of them as being central to most everything I was and everything I did. My difficulty then is knowing what to leave out rather than what to record. In these few pages I will attempt to let you know how she affected my life, she shaped my thinking from early on and how her drive and enthusiasm for what she was as a traveller not only affected me but also the lives of countless others who knew and loved her. So it was with great pleasure and no shortage of pride that I put down on paper what Belle Stewart meant to me (to keep in line with my own heart, I'll refer to her as 'Ma' from now on).

If someone were to ask me to highlight a specific time period which had special meaning to me it would have to be the time we spent living in New Alyth back in the mid to late Sixties. We all lived together on the same tenement row with cousins, our uncle and auntie and Ma and Da. Life was never a bed of roses as we fought an ongoing battle with those who were less than sympathetic to the travelling cause and culture. Nevertheless, I have the fondest memories of my life there. A number of important things spring to mind about my relationship with Ma that I've never forgotten. Just little things to an adult, but to a child they were building-blocks for my future. Like the times she would let us bairns make toast at the fire using the long pitch-fork-type forks with our sleeves pulled over our hands to stop the heat getting to us. I loved it. I also loved cleaning the grate and polishing the multitude of brass ornaments, plates and candlesticks that adorned the fireplace. Ma made them my job and though I was not always in the mood for doing any of them, the fact that she was always full of praise for my efforts made me feel ten feet tall. But by far my favourite job I did for her was to go for logs to the sawmill at the end of the street with an old wheelbarrow Da had. Every time she asked me to do something for her, especially going for the logs, I felt like I was the only person on the earth she could rely upon to get the job done. Her ability to encourage me was all that was needed to set me off. I can remember the day I pushed that barrow full of logs all the way down the street without taking a break. I felt like a world champion that day. Ma may never have realised what effect these small challenges were having upon me but they put something of a work ethic into me that is still a very strong motivation for me to this day.

The folk music was something else. The ceilidhs were as frequent as the visitors who came from all parts of the globe to listen to her stories and hear her sing. Recording equipment strung over their shoulders, they'd pile out of their cars and fight to see who could get through the door first. Well that's how it seemed to a nine-year-old who wondered what all the fuss was about. I mean this was just Ma and Da, my mum and my aunt. Who were all these folk anyway? Over the years, of course, I eventually came to recognise that some of them were world-famous musicians and entertainers. I would sit up till all hours with my brother Ian and sister Heather, eyes red with sleep but never giving in. Ma's voice was like a bell, clear and distinct. She was well-named. She took centre stage, no doubt about it. Her incredible personality and energy never let up as she moved from one song to the next, cracking jokes here and there some of which I later discovered were x-rated – 'You bairns should be in yer beds anyway,' she used to say.

The respect I gained for her over these earlier years was really just the beginning of what was to grow into an admiration that would last a lifetime. As a larger-than-life person who loved me deeply, I never felt anything but safe when I was in her company. I can honestly say that I can't remember a single example of her raising her voice or her hand to me in anger. Not that I never saw her angry of course. She and Da had their moments. I remember the day he arrived home alone from Dundee when they were living in Old Rattray. Nothing unusual about that except that both himself and Ma had gone to the city to shop. He sat down and my Auntie Rena asked where her mother was. 'Div I ken?' his usual reply to things which he was not interested in speaking about; and he definitely was not interested in speaking about his wife that day. It appeared they had been arguing on the way home to Blair and he'd had enough, so he stopped the car and put her out. My Auntie Rena had to go and retrieve her. We all thought it was a great laugh at the time though we kept it to ourselves for a while.

Ma had quite a way with words the 'gift o the gab' as she used to say and her sense of humour never left her even when she was struggling to keep touch with reality a bit at the end. She fell over one time outside the YWCA hall in Blair and to everybody's amazement didn't even suffer a bruise. I rushed to pick her up, thinking she'd have gotten a real shock. I needn't have bothered; she looked up at me and said, 'I fell owre my lang feet tae go wi my lang tongue.' Her humour could turn a tragedy into a celebration. That was Ma and we wouldn't have had her any other way.

It was, of course, largely due to this incredible character that people flocked to the family from all over the world to listen to the songs and stories handed down from generation to generation. As a youngster I was unaware of the importance other people were placing on the work my family were investing their time and efforts into in regards to the travelling culture, and in particular their songs and stories. It was this culture, or should I say the danger of losing this culture, that brought interested parties to the Stewarts of Blair. Recording sessions were commonplace in their homes as every facet of this travelling lifestyle became of paramount importance to others. For me, this seemed ironic in many ways when I thought of the terrible treatment we had to go through at times to even be heard at all. However, I was learning that not everyone shared the same negative viewpoints of some of the locals we rubbed shoulders with every day. Gradually I began to witness an outsiders' respect for Ma and the family which began to change the way I thought about what it was to be a traveller. If important people could respect us, perhaps there was hope that we would be accepted by the locals too. It didn't happen overnight but the dark clouds which hounded our progress for many years have certainly given way to clearer skies above Blairgowrie today. I believe that the impact the Stewarts o Blair have had in their generation contributed very much to this change of heart.

There's a verse in the Good Book which reads, 'God resists the proud but exalts the humble.' It reminds me of one of the things Ma said to me just a few years before she went to a better place: 'The Good Lord was born in a stable wi nothing but some animals fir company and was laid in a bed of straw just like some o oor folk.' What struck me about her words was her sincerity. By this time thoughts of eternity were tending to become more serious to her she attended our church regularly till it became too difficult for her to do so because of her physical condition. Though she never took the time to explain what she meant by her words she didn't have to because she was telling me something right at the end of her days that touched me deeply. She could relate to humble beginnings, but she could also relate to greatness conceived from humble beginnings as well. Born in a bow tent near Caputh, she often said to me that before her mother would go hawking the houses she would always utter a short prayer: 'May the good Lord go before me.' It seems He always did, for Ma lived to the ripe old age of ninety-two, gained the respect of some of the world's most accomplished folk musicians and entertainers, was honoured by the Queen with a BEM and brought an incredible wealth of joy and pleasure to multitudes all over the world. Yet through it all she never lost her grasp of who she was and where she came from. In fact, at the age of eighty she visited the berry fields of Blair for the last time, to pick them, can you believe! I might be accused of being biased but to me that's what greatness is all about, and to me Ma was a great lady.

If she were with us today I would simply want to say to her in closing, thank you, Ma. I love you more than I could ever have said. You fashioned me in so many ways. You loved me, and cared for me, protected me and provided for me when it was called for. You taught me to laugh at nothing much at all, a real 'winnel strays waggin' (someone who can laugh at anything), and cry at the line of a song. You will remain in my heart and mind for the rest of my life as the best grandmother anyone could wish for. So with the farewell words of Big Willie MacPhee to finish off, I'll put down my pen and simply say, 'I'll see ye when I see ye.'

*

Geordie McIntyre

I first met Belle and Alex in the summer of 1964. My family and I were in Alyth as guests. We were warmly received and enjoyed the best of hospitality. At one point in that weekend visit, I was guided to the nearby River Ericht by Alex and benefited from his knowledge of the trout-fishing. However, my main focus was song and story and in this respect experienced a feast. Time has not dimmed the memory of that ceilidh weekend. Belle was in great form. Her singing and varied repertoire were both impressive and inspirational. She displayed a confidence fuelled, I'm sure, by a certain pride – pride in her family and not least in her rich heritage. Her natural grace was coupled to a finely honed infectious good humour.

That memorable first meeting was followed by many more, both in Glasgow and Alyth. One weekend at Alyth, I was taken to meet Alex's sister Jean Thomson and her family at Ferryden (Montrose) and during the ceilidh I recorded a valuable fragment of 'Susie Pye' (Young Beichan, Child 53) sung by Jean. It was Belle who had previously alerted me to this rarity sung by Jean and I was not disappointed.

Later, in 1976, I had the honour to write the sleeve notes for Belle's acclaimed first solo album, 'Queen Amang the Heather'. This apt title mirrored the song of that name and, at another level, her regal contribution to our song tradition. It was a privilege to have known her.

★

This obituary, written by Sheila Miller, a great friend of our family, first appeared in *The Guardian* on 29 September 1997.

Sheila Miller

A Free-born Woman of the Travelling People

Belle Stewart, who has died aged ninety-one, was one of the great interpreters of Scottish traditional song, and one of few to have been officially honoured: she received the British Empire Medal in 1981 for services to traditional music.

Belle was born, into a family of Scottish travellers, in a small bow tent by the side of the River Tay at Caputh, a few miles from Blairgowrie, where she was to live for most of her life. When she was seven months old, her father died, and it became impossible for the family to continue travelling full time. They settled in town and scraped a living by working as fruit-pickers and tattie-howkers (potato-pickers).

Life was hard, but there was always singing and storytelling in the family, and Belle learned many songs that had been handed down orally some for centuries. 'You'd just sit round the fire with all these long ballads, and learn the words and the tune,' Belle told one interviewer. But she was literate, and, as a girl, learned more songs from broadsides and songsheets.

In 1925, she married Alex Stewart, another traveller and a fine piper. The couple travelled in Scotland and Ireland, with Belle learning songs from other travellers. She also wrote songs about the lives of travellers and farm workers, setting them to traditional tunes.

The best known of her own songs 'The Berry Fields o Blair', about the varied people who came to work in Blairgowrie during the fruit-picking season was picked up by other singing travellers, and in 1954 was collected from one of them by Hamish Henderson of Edinburgh's School of Scottish Studies. When the school set out to find the author of the song, the search led to Blairgowrie and Belle.

So the family recorded and, as the Stewarts o Blair, they began to perform at concerts. Meeting the singer and folklorist Ewan MacColl led to many performances in England, and to their voices being used in MacColl's and Charles Parker's famous broadcast works (later issued on record), the *Radio Ballads*. Their *The Travelling People* reflected Belle's own family history. In the late 1980s, a few years before MacColl's own death, he published a book about the Stewart family, *Doomsday in the Afternoon*.

Alex Stewart died in 1980, but Belle and her daughters continued performing in the US and other parts of the world. Hamish Henderson wrote that the Stewarts 'rank high among the singing families of Europe'. Belle recorded a solo album, *Queen Amang the Heather*, as well as several with her family.

She is survived by her two daughters, Cathie and Sheila.

★

Timothy Neat

> Belle Stewart o the Stewarts o Blair, the Queen Amang the
> Heather.
> Belle Stewart and Alex, may their line and their fame never
> die.

I first met Belle in Yeaman Street, Rattray, in 1976. It was August, in a year of much sun, but there were still a few rasps left in the drills and I was making the film *The Summer Walkers* about the Highland travellers. Hamish Henderson had put me onto the Stewarts of Blair. 'No film,' he said, 'can be made about Scotland's travelling people without them; the Perthshire Stewarts are one of the great musical dynasties of Europe. Music flows through them like water o'er the Falls o Lenzie; they'll take you up to see Big Willie MacPhee . . .' And so I went up from Fife and very welcome I was made by Belle and her family. Soon we were down by Erichtside on Thomson's farm and the Stewarts were into the dreels like hounds, Belle and Alex, John the eldest son, Cathie and Sheila, wee Rob Roy MacGregor and a great following of bairns, purple with the woad of the berries.

I was working without funds or professional support and without synchronised sound, but I felt in my element. With a hand-held Bolex I kept pace with the pickers, abreast of hands floating through the sun-dappled leaves, alert to the throw of glances, the swinging of buckets and the smiles. Happy was I then, and later I went out to the Halfway Hoose at Blacklaw, where Sheila told me I would find one of the last of the old-style berry-picker encampments. Largesse, big dogs, beautiful children, a small Shetland in foal and, with my daughter Mary, everywhere I went I was asked into bivvy, tent and caravan. Here was life as told in the tale, here was Strathmore shimmering in a heat-haze of sun, wood-smoke and the fire of good crack. Drunk as a lord on pleasure and plenty, the shackles fell from me. Taking up a handful of dust from the field's edge, I saw the walls o the stardie crumble and in the distance, far distant, I heard it – the sound of the pipes! The Stewarts were returning. *Redeat.*

That September, I began editing *The Summer Walkers* into order. No easy task! I worked on a hand-cranked editor in my son's bedroom in Wormit, and I used Belle's great song 'The Berry Fields o Blair' to carry the East Perthshire sections of the film. It is a song with the ease and naturalness of great poetry and its rhythms are as if born to firm movement. Belle's daughter Sheila makes an even bigger contribution to the film: her stunning rendition of 'Jock Stewart' has spine-tingling power and her version of Ewan MacColl's rebel son, 'Move Along Shift', carries the life of the MacKenzies of Fortingall back to Paleolithic times. And, as so often in life, both Sheila and Belle gave their all for a song for their love of life, their sense of the comradeship which, across millennia, carried mankind before the daze of hard cash. The great refrain in 'Jock Stewart', 'I'm a man youse don't meet every day', evokes images and ideas that sum up the heroic element in traveller life. For centuries, the Stewarts of Blair have been part of the tapestry of Scots life and Belle, bedecked in the red of the Stewart tartan, carried the tradition like a flame.

I remember Belle telling me how she was born on the banks of the Tay, after a long labour, on a day when her father found a fine pearl and sold it well. It was a sign of good luck and with five pounds in his pocket, next day, the family headed north, over the high pass, to Braemar for the Highland Games. It was a fitting beginning to the life of a woman who would become the matriarch of the great Stewart clan. What Rome was to the Romans, roaming is to the travelling people. As all Roman roads led to Rome, so the road of the travellers leads to the Highlands. Romance was in their breath and in their understanding.

On the day of Alex Stewart's funeral, Belle took me by the

hand and led me into the small bedroom where her dear husband lay in his open coffin. His head and face seemed small, his skin was dark and stretched tight over noble cheekbones, his nose markedly hooked in the detumescence of death. He looked like a pharaoh, a mummy, still perfect after 4,000 years. I silently blessed his memory and the great continuum he was part of, and went out into the sunlight deeply moved and strangely exhilarated. Here was death of life and life in death. His clan was with him, his offspring gathered in their dozens around him. Belle and Sheila were beside me, Hamish was with us. It was a moment of time and, looking back, I can see that this scene helped inspire me to open the film *The Tree of Liberty* with an image of the hook-nosed Serge Hovey lying in his bedroom cell in Pacific Palisades, contemplating life and death, Jean Redpath's voice and Robert Burns' words as though he was a pharaoh in his tomb. And the ramifications of that moment in Yeaman Street do not end there because there are good reasons to believe that this film was a major inspiration to Michael Ondaatje when he conceived his novel, *The English Patient*, which later became one of the great films of modern cinema. (Ondaatje and I spoke at length about Hovey, about Hamish, about the travellers, about Jock Townsley on the Anzio beachhead.) From small acorns, mighty oaks grow.

When Alex's body was later taken to the cemetery at Alyth, I found a place at the back of a thick crowd of mourners. Belle, Sheila and Cathie and their families were at the grave's edge. The final prayers were said. Suddenly, as the body of the dead man began to be lowered into the earth, Sheila and Cathie flung their arms to the sky as one and a great cry of anguish came from them. It was a cry of despair and a song; it was a keening welling up from the deep past in the congnach of that moment. And the two daughters flung themselves forward onto the coffin in a last farewell that was also an attempt to claw their father back into the light he was then leaving forever. Here was true mourning, as in ancient days, an archetypal moment that, whilst I live, I shall not forget. These hands against the sky, those towering, keening cries, it was a scene like that captured by Titian and Caravaggio in their fantastic paintings of the entombment of Christ. There are events beyond the span of time.

Back in Blairgowrie at the funeral feast, I met Stewarts and travellers from all over Scotland and I remember in particular the faces of the Robertsons of Aberdeen, Alex's cousins and uncles, Jeannie Robertson's people. I noticed especially the old men with their tanned faces, the skin like fine parchment stretched over the high cheekbones, the crow's-feet smiling around the eyes shaped, long ago, by snow and wind and hunting skills that Siberia, alone, still knows. Here were the heirs of Europe's oldest peoples bearing witness to one of their own. Robertsons, MacGregors, Stewarts, hunter-gatherers, singers, shamans, still refusing, still unable 'to mak an end to their very auld sang'.

Some time after Alex's funeral, Belle wrote Hamish Henderson a letter: 'I've been a bit mixed up lately, Hamish, I didn't break down any time at all at Alex's funeral because I didn't believe he was away but, over the last months, it's hit me very hard . . . ye ken, Hamish, there's nae missin the water till the well runs dry and tae mak matters worse I got my phone cut off . . . Have you any tapes of Alex's stories? I could listen to him and feel he was still with me. I don't think, Hamish, I'm goin a bit queer, oh no I would just like tae listen to Alex . . . I'll have to close my hands are sore (arthritis . . .). Your auld freen Belle.'

Belle's mention of the telephone there reminds me of a strange event that occurred in the late 1980s. We had spoken on the phone and, for some reason, the line between our two houses stayed open. When I tried to make another call, all I could hear was the sound of Belle's kitchen and much singing! The Stewarts' telephone was off the hook and permanently linked to mine. Several times throughout the day, and evening, I checked the line and, hour after hour, they were still at it! Singing, always singing! Talk about a singing family, talk about life as an endless ceilidh. The Stewarts of Blair are proof that music, song and story are so deeply part of traveller life that nothing will silence these custodians of Scotland's song! As the saying goes, 'you can tak the traveller aff the road but ye can niver tak the road oot o the traveller'.

Belle didn't only sing songs, she made songs: one very famous, some now lost or forgotten. One unknown song I have tells the story of how Belle and Alex were taken to the Sheriff Court in Perth, accused of having unsanitary toilet facilities for the pickers working in the berry fields that the family owned in the fifties. Hamish got Lionel Daiches, the distinguished Edinburgh lawyer, to defend them and Belle was inspired to begin writing a ballad on the evening following their first day in court:

On the first day of October that day of renown
Lionel Daiches and Hamish they came to Perth Town
To defend a poor traveller who'd committed an offence
By allowing some tinkers to earn a few pence.

It happened in Blairgowrie in the month of July
When these poor people their luck came to try.
But the law was against them which was a hard case
For years they have come to that very same place.

Now my case it was opened about two o'clock
When Daiches got in there he sure made them rock
For they listened with amazement at what he did say
And the case was put back to a fortnight today.

But I think I'd be pleased if my case came to trial
Just to sit there and see the queer looks on their dial
For their by-laws are hopeless as Daiches just said
So I'll forget all about them and go to my bed.

I don't know whether Belle ever completed the ballad but at the second hearing the Stewarts won their case and, even in fragmentary form, the ballad like her balladic life is part of the folk history of twentieth-century Scotland.

Belle Stewart was a wonderful woman: kind to me, fiercely protective of her family and brave for the good of all mankind. I remember her travelling to Dumfries to sing against the planners who sought to prohibit the memorial sculpture being erected in

Hugh MacDiarmid's honour at Langholm. I remember her debating with John Berger, John Byrne and Liz Lochhead in Dundee. Their theme was 'Nationalism and the Making of Art in Small Countries' and it was Belle's voice (with Sheila and Cathie) that stole the show. Today, Belle Stewart might well have ended up a university professor. In her day, she was fated to remain a traveller. She lived and died poor, but did she do worse? In life, Belle Stewart embodies much of what is best about Scotland and it's great that she lived long enough to know herself loved and honoured far and wide.

Belle liked to quote Burns' saying, 'an auld freen is the best o aa freens' and I'll end by quoting a letter she wrote to Hamish, one of her oldest and best friends, in April 1985. 'Dear Hamish I am looking through some old letters and cards and I came on one that you must have sent at Xmas and inside was an Irish blessing. Well, it's really good and I got the best blessing of all and it was in Ireland, and that was where I met Alex and also got married. In Ireland. I'll keep the paper blessing always.'

And in Scotland, Belle Stewart is a name that will always be remembered.

★

Ann Neilson

Of course, I knew who Belle Stewart was even before I ever saw her, and I knew about the Stewarts o Blair, but the fact that actually I knew nothing was abundantly clear when I first saw her performance at a wee folk club somewhere in Perthshire in the early eighties. I have no memory of what she sang, but I still remember the command that she exercised in that room. She was a singer with complete confident ownership of her repertoire and a justifiable pride in her heritage; she also knew her audience inside out, giving them what she wanted, and what they wanted. (This is a trick that other singers might do well to learn.)

The next time I saw Belle was shortly after she was awarded

the BEM from the Queen, when she appeared in a revised Blairgowrie Festival. There was a concert in the town hall that had a raised stage. When Belle finally came on, it was to deliver a stunning set. She stood there like a 'Queen Amang the Heather' in her tartan dress, with the most elegant legs, and didn't she know it! She radiated life and energy, flirting with her voice, her eyes and, of course, her ankles. The audience was putty in her hands.

The last time I saw Belle was at her ninetieth birthday party the family had organised in the old jute mill in Rattray. Many great and famous singers came to pay their respects to Belle. There was a TV crew there as well, filming everything. Belle sat in a wheelchair looking surprised and a bit confused at what was going on, and there was even more noise and excitement when the buffet was unveiled. It was a feast for a king: fresh strawberries and rasps picked that morning and trays of the most wonderful food you could imagine. Everybody in the room either played an instrument or sang a song. Belle's head was nodding and hung down as if she was asleep. Then I started to sing 'The Berry Fields o Blair'. Halfway through, her head came up and she joined me to finish the song.

I count myself privileged to have met and known such a graceful and dignified lady, with that mischievous twinkle in her eye.

★

Bob Pegg

I knew there was something special about these people when they climbed into the taxi. They seemed monumental, as if they were carved out of stone. I was sixteen, still at school, to it must have been around 1960. Arnold Wesker's Centre 42 circus had come to Nottingham, our town, and we local folk singers had been invited to join the professionals, including Belle and Alex Stewart, Ray Fisher, the Ian Campbell Folk Group and Louis Killen, to perform in pubs, clubs and concert venues around the city.

It was Belle and Alex who shared the taxi with us that rainy night. I recall Belle as being a very handsome and beautifully dressed woman, who, in retrospect, reminds me a bit of the Queen Mum. Of Alex, I remember most vividly the huge pair of knees facing us in the back of that taxi. He was only the second Scotsman I had ever met, and the first to be wearing the kilt. It was also the first time I'd been in the same room as the Highland bagpipes; every concert began with Alex entering from the back and marching up the central aisle to the accompaniment of his own magnificent piping.

Alex's playing and Belle's incomparable singing were highlights of the week when Centre 42 came to town. I remember them vividly as people both dignified and kindly, the perfect ambassadors for the culture of the Scottish travelling people.

★

Peta Webb

I first saw Belle in the mid Sixties when I was a student at Oxford; the Heritage Society booked the Stewarts of Blair, with Belle, Alex (on pipes) and their daughters Cathie and Sheila. They wore Scots Highland dress and were a most impressive and colourful introduction to the song and music of the travelling people. The vivacious singing of mother and daughters together made a lasting impression.

After that, I went to see them as often as I could at clubs and festivals, admiring Sheila's hard-edged voice and Cathie's Irish songs but particularly enjoying Belle's singing. Her lyrical ballads, such as 'Queen Amang the Heather', were sung with exquisite subtlety, with beautiful decorations and long, drawn-out notes. They were a great model when I was developing my own style. But no less memorable was her delivery of bawdy songs like 'The Keyhole in the Door' she clearly relished the naughtiness of this peeping-Tom song. In her neat tailored tartan frock and lace jabot, only Belle could get away with it!

Belle was a great ambassador for the travelling people, through her natural dignity, the power of her performance and her determination to pass on the wisdom of the travelling culture through songs and stories. Her wide repertoire also preserved Scots ballads of the non-travelling people and she sang the cantarach (the music of the pipes expressed as syllables for the voice), carrying on after Alex's death the music of the great champion piper. Her humanity and tolerance of all comes out in her song of experience, 'The Berry Fields o Blair'.

I have a treasured tape of Belle singing at the National Folk Music Festival in 1988, where she sang some of the old sentimental songs (in the company of Sheila and her grandsons Rob Roy and Ian) as well as a lively 'Wish I was Back in Smeraldairye'. It is a wonderful reminder of the many good times she shared with others.

★

Sheena Wellington

I was a great fan of Belle Stewart's singing and songs long before I met her in person. Strangely, though, the when and where of our first introduction has been lost to memory but the impression she made was immediate and lasting.

Belle was a personality; an upright graceful lady who was warm and kind, with a glint of mischief in her eyes. She was, of course, a great singer, but she was also one of the most compelling performers I have ever seen. She could enchant the aristocracy as effortlessly as she could enthral a folk club audience; she could captivate the county and the cottage.

Belle could spot a phoney 200 yards away and her judgments of people were swift, shrewd and seldom wrong. I recall one festival where the director had alternately patronised and snubbed Belle. This pretentious dame had the audacity to demand that I, as MC of the evening concert, 'tell Belle she has to sing tonight because the Lord Lieutenant is coming!' I went to see Belle, knelt beside her, and asked if she would do me the honour of singing at my concert. With that lovely smile, she said, 'For you darling, I'd dance the fan dance in the Wellmeadow!'

I was still raging at the rudeness of the director, but Belle took it in her stride. 'I ken her family history', she said tolerantly, 'and she's always had to try and live it down!'

Not so Belle. She was fiercely proud of her people and the culture that they had carried. She knew the story of her family thoroughly and could tell tales of their doings going back generations. How blessed we are that Belle had the generosity to share so many of the ballads, stories and lore with us.

There was also something of the magical about her. Most of her friends have memories of events which appeared to go beyond mere coincidence. Once, when I was living in St Andrews, I was preparing the house for a gathering of singers. As I dusted my little china keyhanger, it slipped out of my hands and smashed to smithereens. Three hours later, and knowing nothing of this misfortune, Belle arrived with a gift of a brass horseshoe key holder which still had pride of place in my home!

To mark her eightieth birthday, she and Cathie came into my Radio Tay studio. The stories, songs and jokes came thick and fast. I loved it and so did the listeners – it sparked my biggest ever postbag. After the show, we went for a Chinese meal. To my surprise, the waiter suddenly appeared with a beautifully decorated iced sponge cake complete with candles. Belle thought I had staged it. Actually, it had been ordered for another party but had arrived two days early. The manager was happy to give it to the gracious lady who had charmed him. Another slightly spooky Belle moment!

I last saw here at her ninetieth birthday party in Blairgowrie. She was in her last illness and was brought in a wheelchair. She seemed almost asleep but as soon as she saw the crowd of friends waiting, her back became ram-rod straight and she acknowledged us with the grace of the queen of singers that she undoubtedly was. As we sang for her she joined in, those glorious eyes sparkling.

Hundreds were at her funeral, the tributes warm, the feeling that this was the passing of an era and we would not see her like again. Just as they lowered the coffin, six RAF jets in formation roared overhead. Danny Kyle summed it up: 'That's Belle – organising a fly-past for her own funeral!'

Thank you, Belle, for the songs, the stories, the jokes and the memories. And thank you for allowing me the privilege of calling you my friend.

★

Mike Yates

Belle Stewart: A Personal Appreciation

There is a term Outsider Art that is used in the art world and which refers to people, often self-taught artists, who create works of art that are outside the mainstream of the current art movement. If the term were to be used in the world of music and literature, then the names of Belle Stewart and her remark-able family would be up there alongside Rabbie Burns and James Hogg, the Ettrick Shepherd. Belle, like Burns and Hogg, was raised in a society of oral tradition. It is doubtful that, as a child, she would ever have considered the songs, ballads, tales, jokes and riddles that she heard all around her to be anything other than the norm, not realising that the world beyond her travelling community was rapidly forsaking these remarkable, and often ancient, traditions, preferring instead to rely on the book's page, rather than on the understanding of their own ears.

> O, two pretty boys were gaen to the school
> And one evening coming home,
> Said William to John, 'Can you throw a stone,
> Or can you play at ball, at ball,
> Or can you play at ball?'

Belle had the ballad of 'The Twa Brothers' from the singing of her brother, Donald MacGregor. I suspect that neither knew, nor cared, that the story was but a retelling of the ancient Greek legend of Telamon and Peleus, because John and William, the two protagonists in the ballad, were real people so far as Belle and Donald were concerned. Similarly, historians might suggest that the incident described in 'The Bonnie Hoose o Airlie' took place on 7 July 1640. It was another ballad that came partly from Donald and, again, it seems to have transcended historical time, occurring simply 'on a bonnie summer day'.

> It fell on a day, on a bonnie summer day,
> When the corn was ripe and yellow,
> That there fell oot a great dispute
> Between Argyll and Airlie.

I am not trying to say that Belle or Donald were not aware that many of their songs and ballads often had historical provenance, far from it. In fact, Belle learned part of 'The Bonnie Hoose o Airlie' at school and it would seem possible that her teacher would have explained something about the song's historical background to her. Rather, I am saying that when Belle and Donald sang about these people, they perceived them to be as real and as individual as the people who made up their own everyday society. When the English gypsy singer Phoebe Smith was once asked how she thought about her songs, she replied, 'You can imagine . . . I can . . . as well as feeling for them . . . things that happened . . . what they did. I can picture them, you know, in the sorrow parts as well as the happiness. They're *human*.'

There is a Buddhist story about a young man who is given a coat with a valuable jewel hidden within the lining. The man struggles through his life without realising that he is carrying such a treasure with him. I mention this because Belle was just the opposite of this man. Belle was only too aware that she carried a great treasure with her, namely her heritage. Belle Stewart was lucky, in that she was surrounded by other outstanding people throughout her life. Her parents and in-laws were all gifted singers, musicians and storytellers and Belle was proud to pass on all that she had learned to other generations.

I first met Belle, Alex, Cathie and Sheila a year or so before they recorded their beautiful topic album *The Stewarts o Blair* in the mid 1960s. So far as they were concerned, I must have been just another unknown person trying to tap into their traditions. And yet, stranger or not, I was made so welcome that I have never forgotten those first days spent in their company. Belle, regal in bearing and kind in manner, was clearly the matriarch of the family and her guiding hand was ever present in all that they did. Alex, a slightly reserved man, was never prouder than when playing his pipes. And their daughters, Cathie and Sheila, two young girls full of energy and vitality, were forever breaking into song.

The first thing that Belle taught me was the fact that there is far more to a person than just their songs and stories. Belle told of a traveller's life full of hardships and struggles. Yet, strangely enough, she also spoke of a life full of joy, happiness and success. I think that much of the latter came about because the songs and stories that she had heard since childhood had prepared her for all that life could throw at her. Many travellers tell stories about a boy called Jack who often lives with his orphan mother in a poor cottage on the margins of society. No matter what the adventure, Jack always comes out on top, usually because of his own abilities, and that is what Belle and Alex sought to do throughout their lives. Both overcame adversity and both changed the lives of thousands of people who met them and heard them perform their songs and music. Belle certainly had a presence about her when she sang, be it on stage in front of a thousand strangers, or else in the snug surroundings of her own home. When Belle began to sing, people listened.

I am sometimes asked which of the traditional singers and storytellers I have known was the best. And I always reply by saying that, so far as I am concerned, they are all the best. I say this because, like many others, I am only too grateful to these people for not only maintaining their heritage, but also because they were prepared to pass it on to others, making the world a better place. But, with hindsight, I think that the Stewarts, especially Belle and Alex, would really be at the top of any list that I could make. Kind, and generous to a fault, they changed the direction that my life was to take. And, for that, I am eternally grateful.